2nd Edition

HOW TO DO A 1031 EXCHANGE OF REAL ESTATE

Using a 1031 Qualified Intermediary (QI)

Or, how to defer thousands of dollars in **taxes !!**

Edwin V. Horan, MS

Order this book online at www.trafford.com
or email orders@trafford.com

Most Trafford titles are also available at major online book retailers.

Print information available on the last page.

ISBN: 978-1-4907-9996-4 (sc)
ISBN: 978-1-6987-0036-6 (e)

Library of Congress Control Number: 2020904101

Trafford rev. 04/15/2020

 www.trafford.com
North America & international
toll-free: 1 888 232 4444 (USA & Canada)
fax: 812 355 4082

CONTENTS

DEDICATION

This book is dedicated to my family. To my recently passed wife Jane, my two children Bill and Cynthia, and to my four grandsons, Kevin and Max, who are military helicopter pilots, and to Jeff and Will.

ACKNOWLEDGEMENTS

Any book on a subject as technical as IRC Section 1031 requires a great deal of research and study. I wish to acknowledge the authors of a book, updated annually, that I have used extensively over the years.

Mary Foster and the late Jerry Long are the authors of '*Tax-Free Exchanges Under §1031*', the premier text and reference book for real estate, legal and accounting professionals involved in like kind exchanges. Their kind advice and assistance has been graciously given to me on many occasions.

Also, the staff and officers of the Federation of Exchange Accommodators (FEA) receive our special thanks for all of their efforts to keep the membership appraised of the many changes taking place with exchange legislation and IRS rulings. The establishment of the prestigious FEA *Certified Exchange Specialist*® (CES®) program brought national recognition to those professional qualified intermediaries who have demonstrated their knowledge, experience and ethical behavior.

IMPACT OF TAX CUT AND JOBS ACT (TCJA)

In late December 2017, the Congress passed and the President signed the Tax Cuts and Jobs Act (TCJA).

It had a major impact on many areas of taxation and investment.

Section 13303. of the Act amended IRC Section 1031 to eliminate PRIVATE PROPERTY exchanges. It retained REAL PROPERTY (Real Estate) 1031 exchanges.

Major effort by the Federation of Exchange Accommodators (FEA)and other organizations saved the 1031 exchange for real estate.

A copy of the current amended IRC Section 1031 is in the Appendix in the rear of this book.

Chapter 1

WHY DO A 1031 EXCHANGE?

1. **Economic Reasons.** When the owner (taxpayer) wants to better their rental real estate, wishing to move up, to a better economic business opportunity or invest in a better location they will want to do a 1031 exchange. They will want to do a 1031 exchange so that they will have the cash needed to acquire replacement property and continue their investment in the economy. The basic rational for doing a Section 1031 exchange has always been Congress' desire not to impose a tax on theoretical gain when tax payers continue their investment in like-kind property without an intervening actual or constructive receipt of cash or non-like kind property. A like-kind exchange deferral allows a taxpayer to shift to a more productive like-kind property, normally moving up while helping the economy grow.

2. **Other Reasons.** While there are prime economic reasons for doing a 1031 exchange, the following reasons have been culled from the writings of industry leaders.

   - Deferral of taxes when property sold
   - Relocation of investment
   - Keeping all the equity available (no loss to taxes)
   - Consolidation of investments
   - Diversification of investment property
   - No requirement that two parties want each other's property
   - No requirement settlements be simultaneous
   - Few limitations on type of replacement property (real estate for real estate)
   - Less management (DST or triple net)
   - Opportunity for greater cash flow
   - Available leverage when moving up
   - Non depreciable to depreciable
   - Tax – free loan
   - No capital gain recognized on death
   - Heirs inherit property at current FMV
   - Avoidance of 3.8% tax
   - Availability of reverse exchange
   - Conversion to principal residence

3. **Why Not Do An Exchange?** If you are selling investment real estate and plan to purchase replacement real estate in the near future, it is foolish not to consider a tax deferred like-kind exchange and take advantage of Uncle Sam's tax-free loan. Since every investor has a unique situation (such as having suspended passive losses), they should discuss any planned exchange with their CPA or tax advisor.

If you go to Calculate Gains on top menu at www.1031.us you may automatically compute the tax due if you were to sell the property, and the 1031 exchange reinvestment requirements for a 1031 exchange.

Chapter 2

HISTORY OF LIKE-KIND EXCHANGES

1. **Old Tax Law.** What surprises most investors is that a law covering the exchange of property has been around for so long. When the income tax was created by Congress in 1918 all gained was taxed. However, in 1921 Congress created Section 1031 predecessor and it relatively unchanged over the years.

2. **Four Exchange Periods.** When we look at exchanging today, historically we can divide the time into four periods. The first period is from the start to 1979. The second period is from 1979 to 1990, with the third period running from 1979 to 2017. The fourth period started with the passage of the 'Tax Cut and Jobs Act' (TCJA). This legislation restricted 1031 exchanges to real property (i.e. real estate)

3. **First Exchange Period.** This period which starts from the early start in 1921 extends to 1979 is a very quiet period in exchanging in which only a few exchanges were completed. Those investors who had sharp professional attorneys and CPAs were the ones who made use of exchanging. This period came to an end with the United States Ninth Circuit Court decision in 1979 to approve deferred exchanges. Their decision, the famous Starker cases, established an important precedent. It basically said taxpayers could transfer their property to one party and receive the replacement property later from a third party, This, set off a wave of exchanges particularly on the West Coast.

4. **Second Exchange Period.** During the second period from 1979 to 1990 there was great deal of action by Congress to keep up with the Ninth Circuit Court decision in the 1979 Starker case. In recognition of the Starker decision, Congress modified Section 1031 of the Internal Revenue Code to 'codify' the deferred exchange as we know it today. In the Deficit Reduction Act of 1984 the Congress also established the 45-day identification and the 180-day exchange periods. The Tax Reform Act of 1986 had a major impact on residential investments and lead to the growth of tax-deferred exchanges. This act eliminated preferential capital gains treatment, enacted 'passive loss' and eliminated accelerated depreciation for real estate. These changes almost eliminated the tax benefits of owning investment real estate. The tax-deferred like-kind exchange became one of the few remaining benefits for real estate investors. The Congress and IRS have continued over these past decades to modify the exchange rules. In the 1989 change to the IRC it was decreed that foreign and domestic property was not considered like kind and thus

could not be exchanged. The restrictions on related party exchanges (the addition of Section 1031(f) were also established.

5. Third Exchange Period. We can say that during the third period that Congressional action to modify the Internal Revenue Code 1031 was very active. Beginning in the third period in 1990 the U.S. Treasury and the Internal Revenue Service became very active with the publication of the new exchange regulations, Revenue Procedures and Private Letter Rulings. The exchange ball really started to roll with the draft publication in May of 1990 in the Federal Register of the proposal to add regulations for deferred exchanges. There were many public comments and a hearing was held on September 5, 1990. After consideration of the comments submitted the IRS adopted and published the final regulations for 1031 exchanges in June 1991.

While many regulation captions appear under Section 1.1031-0 of the final regulations the regulatory sections must written about and discussed is Sections 1.1031(k)-1, "Treatment of deferred exchanges". In addition to the publication of the exchange regulations in 1990 there have many Revenue Procedures and Private Letter Rulings published on 1031 activities during this period. A summary of the regulatory changes considered important are listed below. Many of these are discussed in detailed in this book.

Revenue Procedure 2000-37, established procedures for accommodation of **reverse exchanges**. This was amended by Revenue Procedure 2004-51 to restrict taxpayer ownership of replacement property within 180 days of transfer to exchange accommodator titleholder (EAT).

Revenue Procedure 2002-22, provided criteria for getting a **TIC ruling**.

Revenue Ruling 2002-83 was published in November 2002 to clarify the purchase of the replacement property from a **related party**.

Revenue Ruling 2004-86 states a beneficial interest in a Delaware Statutory Trust (DST) is an interest in real property and thus qualifies in a 1031 exchange.

Revenue Procedure 2005-14 was published in February 2005 permits exclusion of gain where appropriate under both **Section 121** and under **Section 1031**.

Revenue Procedure 2005-27 provided separate instruction for exchangers in section 17 of the procedure for taxpayers in a presidentially **declared disaster** area.

Private Letter Ruling (PLR) 2004-4002 confirmed that Section 1031(f) did not apply if the related person seller is also doing an exchange and **not cashing out.**

Effective in April 1994, the regulation 1.1031(k) was amended be adding paragraph -1(j)(2) which coordinated **installment sale** and like-kind exchanges.

In February 2002, Treasury Decision 89982, Section 1.1031(k)-1(k)(4) was amended to **excuse bank affiliates** from the disqualification rules.

The October 2004 the American Jobs Creation Act (H.R. 4520) amended IRC Section 121(d) to require that a principal residence acquired in a 1031 exchange must be **owned** for 5 years before it qualifies for exclusion of gain under IRC Section 121(a).

Starting with the 1991 tax return the IRS established Form 8824 for reporting like-kind exchanges.

6. Fourth Exchange Period. Historically, the action in the TCJA to amend the basic 1031 law to eliminate 'personal property' 1031 exchanges and allow only 'real property' (real estate) 1031 exchanges starts a new era. The impact of this major change has not yet been fully evaluated. The IRS has not fully revised its regulations covering the subject.

7. National Organization. The Federation of Exchange Accommodators (FEA) is the national trade association organized to represent professionals who conduct like-kind exchanges under Internal Revenue Code Section 1031. Members primarily include Qualified Intermediaries (QIs) who follow an industry wide code of ethics. FEA is the voice for the 1031 exchange industry and works to educate consumers on effectively using 1031 exchanges to defer capital gains tax. One important task the FEA has undertaken is the establishment of the Certified Exchange Specialist (CES)® program. To be designated a CES an individual must prove at least three years full time experience and pass a very tough examination on 1031 exchange rules. In addition, a CES must complete 20 hours of approved exchange continuing education every two years. For a list of Certified Exchange Specialist in your area go to the CES web site www.1031.ces.org.

[The most comprehensive §1031 history is that by M.E. Kornhauser, that is in Vol.60, of the Southern California Law Review]

Chapter 3

CRITERIA FOR AN EXCHANGE

1. **What is a 1031 Exchange?** A 1031 exchange is called by many names, including: a tax deferred exchange, a like-kind exchange, a tax free exchange, and a swap. There are many types of real estate transactions that meet the criteria, and therefore are eligible to do a 1031 exchange. To define a 1031 exchange it is best for us to quote directly from the IRS regulation 1.1031(k)-1(a).

   *"a deferred exchange is defined as an exchange in which pursuant to an **agreement**, the taxpayer **transfers property held** for productive use in a trade or business or for investment (the 'relinquished property') and **subsequently** receives property **to be held** either for productive use in a trade or business or for investment (the 'replacement property')".*

2. **Criteria for a 1031 Tax Deferred Exchange.** In addition to the IRS regulations the Internal Revenue Code (IRC) 1031 spells out criteria to be met for the property to be tax deferred. Basically these are:

   a. Both properties must be in the United States, or
   b. Both properties must be outside the U.S.
   c. For the Relinquished Property(ies) the property currently must be used by the exchanger for <u>investment, business or production of income.</u>

      *It is **not** important how the buyer plans to use the property!!*

   d. For the **Replacement Property**(ies) the exchanger must hold the new property <u>for investment, business and/or production of income.</u>

      *It is **not** important how the property is currently being used by the seller!!*

   e. The replacement property(ies) must be identified in 45 days after transfer of ownership of the relinquished
   f. The replacement property(ies) must be settled/owned in 180 days (or the tax due date, including extension, if earlier).

It is not important that a purchaser buying an investor's property plans to use it as a personal residence; or that the property the exchanger acquires is currently being used as a personal residence, an investment or business property. The property to be acquired can be currently used in any status - business, investment, dealer or personal.

The status of the currently owned property and the use the exchanger will make of the acquired replacement property is what is important!

3. What is Like-Kind? A like-kind exchange of real estate is a 1031 exchange or tax deferred exchange. Some everyday rules to define a like-kind exchange are:

1) The relinquished property and replacement property must be like-kind to qualify as a § 1031 exchange.
2) One kind or class of property may not be exchanged for a property of a different kind or class.
3) Like-kind refers to the nature and/or character of the property, not its quality or grade.
4) Property must be held for productive use in a trade, or business, or for investment.
5) Real estate is generally like-kind with all other real estate.

4. What Section 1031 Does Not Cover. We know that §1031 provides for the exchange of a business or investment property for any other business or investment property. It is just as important to know what §1031 does not cover.

First, a current **Principal Residence** cannot be included in an exchange under the provisions of §1031. Nor does a replacement property to be immediately converted to a principal residence or personal use qualify as a like kind replacement property.

Second, **dealer property** cannot be exchanged under IRC 1031 provisions. Dealer property is property held for resale and is considered inventory. A developer who purchases and resells lots could be considered a dealer. Also a contractor who buys and renovates homes and then immediately sells them could also be considered a dealer.

Third, **partnership interests** may not be exchanged under §1031. Many small investment or business properties are owned by partnerships. If title to the property is in the name of the partnership (example: "Smith Properties Partnership"), then the entire partnership must do the exchange. Individual partners may not exchange their interest because they have an interest in the partnership, and not in the real estate. However, if the property is deeded to individuals, as say "tenants-in-common", and they do not file a partnership tax return, then each tenant in common owner may exchange their separate interest in the real estate, or pay the tax as they desire. Also, partners may use IRC Section 761(a) to elect out of the partnership and become eligible to exchange their interest in the property. Investors in a partnership should get tax and legal advice before engaging in an exchange.

5. Additional Qualifying Exchanges. Most exchanges are simple ones which meet the criteria above. However, there are exchanges that have special rules associated with them:

> **Second home or vacation property.** Most tax practitioners and the Tax Court agree that when a second home is used exclusively for personal use, it does not qualify for a §1031 exchange. The difference in opinion occurs when the second home or vacation property is also rented out. There is little question that when the personal use of the vacation rental property is limited to 14 days or 10% of the days actually rented, whichever is greater, the property qualifies for a 1031 exchange. After many years of urging, the IRS published Revenue Procedure 2008-16 (copy in Appendix)which provides taxpayers with a 'safe harbor' under which a dwelling unit will qualify for a 1031 exchange as a property held for productive use in a trade or business or for investment even though a taxpayer occasionally uses the dwelling for personal purposes.

There are other situations pertaining to vacation or second homes, not covered by the revenue procedure, which may still qualify the owner to do a 1031 exchange. This is such an important topic we cover it in a separate chapter.

Reverse exchanges. The Section 1031 law requires that the relinquished property be transferred and then subsequently acquire the replacement property. The exchanger cannot own both properties at the same time. The IRS recognized the need for taxpayers to be able to arrange transactions where the taxpayer can get control of a replacement property before they have transferred their relinquished property. In 2000 the IRS published Revenue Procedure 2000-37 which provides "safe harbor" procedures for the accommodation of reverse exchanges using an Exchange Accommodation Titleholder (EAT). See Chapter 10 in this book for a complete explanation of the reverse exchange procedure.

Important - A replacement property may be placed under contract at any time - however, under §1031 you may not go to settlement on the replacement property until settlement on the relinquished property. Thus, the need for a reverse exchange and the revenue procedure.

Related party exchanges. In 1989 the 1031 law was amended to add subsection 1031(f) which places restrictions on exchanges between related parties. Over the last couple of years there have been a number of Private Letter Rulings (PLR) to help clarify, particular type related party exchanges. A separate chapter covers subject.

> **Shared equity exchanges**. Investors can be co-owners with home owners. For many years with the appreciation of real estate and now facing a credit tightening on loans many first time home buyers find buying a home on their own is not financially possible. They need to look to others for financial help. As an example,

a couple may look to parents to become co-owners with them to buy a new home. If the parents agree to be co-owners and the new couple use the home as a primary residence, the parent's co-ownership of the home is considered a second home or personal use property because family is personally using the property. If the parents are exchangers, and want to help the couple, they must own business or investment property, not a personal use property. When an investor rents a dwelling unit to any person who will be using it as their primary residence the rent must be at fair market value.

An investor can exchange into a residence with the purchase of the property with the other owner(s) who are to be the owner-occupants. Each party, for example the young couple, and the other co-buyer(s), the owner-investor, maintain all their tax breaks and advantages thanks to Uncle Sam. This joint ownership is controlled by a mandatory **Shared Equity Financing Agreement (SEFA)** and other documentation. Under these agreements the couple pay the investor co-owner(s) a fair rental value for their share of the property. For example, the SEFA would define the period and terms of co-ownership, establish the split of profits when the property is sold, and/or when the occupants can buy out the owner-investor. If the occupants buy out the owner-investor the owner-investor can do a 1031 exchange, because they own business/investment property. If the parties do not have a SEFA the investor may not claim to be holding a business or investment property and the co-purchase would not have qualified as an exchange.

Tenants-in-common exchanges(TIC). During the real estate boom of the 2000's investors were joining together in partnerships or joint ventures to purchase properties trying to take advantage of the investment opportunity. Investors who do 1031 exchanges need to take title to real estate versus joining into a partnership. The IRS issued Revenue Procedure 2002-22 to give guidance to investment groups who might ask the IRS for a private letter ruling on their particular ownership structure of a transaction where owners would hold tenant in common interests and not deemed to be in a partnership. The IRS gave 15 criteria that TIC agreements must have to qualify as real estate interest. This permitted real estate investors to purchase interests in a TIC property, which are primarily commercial properties. Following this IRS revenue procedure in 2002 the TIC industry exploded into a multibillion-dollar industry. The TIC structure permitted smaller investors to exchange out of smaller properties into much larger properties with others and take advantage of completely new investment opportunities that they individually would not have been able to enter into. For example, an individual investor may exchange a single-family rental property for a small TIC interest in a shopping center. In most cases the TIC property is professionally managed and there is little day to day involvement by the investor. With the downturn in the real estate market over the last few years many of the TIC properties failed and investors faced losses.

Delaware statuary trust (DST). In Revenue Ruling 2004-86 the IRS recognized that a taxpayer may exchange qualifying real property for an interest in a Delaware Statuary Trust (DST) in a § 1031 exchange. The DST is set up under Delaware law and is used by investors who wish reduced management responsibilities. The revenue ruling provides specific IRS guidance and conditions for a DST. A DST provides that while the owner does not receive a deed, he does have a percentage ownership in a trust that owns real property. There is no limit on the number of investors in a DST. The only right of an investor is to receive DST distributions. The investor may not have any voting rights. Since lenders only look to the DST as the single borrower, versus looking to each tenant in common owner. The DST is replacing the TIC investment route for many investors. The DST investment structure has some specific restrictions on its activity. There are prohibitions on the trustee of the DST which are called the "seven deadly sins". An investor needs to make sure they have good counsel when looking to invest in a DST. While the use of a QI is still required an exchanger should fully understand from their attorney or tax advisor what they will receive and what their rights are in a DST.

Foreign real property exchanges. Real property located in the United States and real property located outside of the United States are not considered like-kind property. Foreign real property is real property not located in a state or the District of Columbia. A foreign property may be exchanged for other foreign property. This restriction is imposed by IRC Section 1031(h). A foreigner may do a 1031 exchange of a property in the United States for another in this country and also deferred tax payments. Special withholding rules apply for foreign owners so U.S. buyers need to be especially wary.

Leasehold interests. An investor can exchange out of or into a long-term leasehold interest. In order for a lease to be considered real property and thus eligible for a like-kind exchange some additional rules relative to the lease must be observed. The long-term lease must have at least thirty years remaining in the term, including any extensions. For example, when exchanging into a 25 year lease, with two 5 year extensions, the IRS considers this a 35 year lease for 1031 purposes. In addition to a QI, an investor exchanging into a long-term leasehold interest should consult with a CPA and /or attorney to be sure it qualifies as a 1031 exchange.

Chapter 4

TAX IMPACT OF A SALE

1. **Sale Without a 1031 Exchange.** The first step to decide if we should simply sell and pay the tax, or exchange an investment property is to estimate the tax that will be due and the net sales proceeds after tax.

Many investors selling a property do not realize that not only is profit taxed but there is a **recapture** of depreciation, and they will most likely incur other taxes.

> **If you do a 1031 exchange, you defer capital gains tax, including recapture of depreciation. You avoid the addition of other added taxes, including the**
>
> **3.8% NII, .09% Medicare tax and AMT**

To see the automatic impact of a proposed sale simply go to www.1031.us for the REC on-line exchange analysis form. On top menu select 'Calculate Gain'. It provides a form for an excellent automatic computation of property basis, taxable gain, gain tax due, proceeds and exchange reinvestment requirements. Also, at the end of this Chapter is simple form to estimate Taxable Gain if property is SOLD.

The sale profit will be added to your regular income, and thus this higher income may dictate additional taxes.

2. **Income Tax Brackets.** The tax rates on long-term capital gain have not changed. But the Congress decided in the law to set separate income brackets for the different capital gain tax rates. These tax brackets are subject to inflation adjustments. For 2020 the brackets are:

Tax Rate	Income if single	Income if married, filing jointly
0%	Up to $40,000	Up to $80,000
15%	$40,001 to $441,450	$80,001 to $496,600
20%	All over $441,450	All over $496,000

Income from the sale of collectibles, gold, silver, and similar items is taxed at 28%.

3. Recapture of Depreciation/Section 1250 Gain. All depreciation taken or allowed on real property must be recaptured and taxed upon sale. For Section 1250 property, the tax is total depreciation taken/authorized times 25%. For all other type property on which depreciation is taken the tax is the standard income tax rate of the owner times all the depreciation taken. (The 25% rate cannot be greater than the tax payers actual final rate – i.e. thus it may be less than 25%). This tax is computed on the 'Schedule D Tax Worksheet' or similar form.

4. 3.8% NII Tax Rules and Thresholds The 3.8% net investment income (NII) tax or 0.9% Medicare tax were not revoked, nor were the threshold amounts increased. <u>If your income is over the threshold amounts</u>, the amount you will owe is based on the lesser tax on your total net investment income or the amount of your MAGI that exceeds $200,000 for individuals, $250,000 for couples filing jointly, or $125,000 for spouses filing separately. By definition, MAGI includes your adjusted gross income (AGI), wages from work, net investment income, qualified distributions from a retirement plan, such as a traditional IRA, 401(k), or 403(b), and any foreign earned income exclusion you may have had.

In other words, you'll owe the 3.8% tax on all your investment income, OR, if your wages alone already are higher than the income thresholds, you'll owe tax on the lesser of net investment income OR tax on portion of MAGI that exceeds the thresholds.

First, you must have MAGI over the threshold amount, or you do not have to pay any 3.8% NII tax. Second, if you have a high MAGI above thresholds suggest you compute both taxes and select the one that is **lesser.** *Total net investment income, including capital gains, times 3.8% to get the first possible tax; then multiply MAGI amount over thresholds by 3.8% to get second possible tax, then select the lesser as the additional tax you will have to pay.*

Real estate sellers, as high-income taxpayers, may still be subject to one or both of two taxes that took effect in 2013 to help pay for health care. One on investment income and the other on earned income.

5. Additional 0.9% Medicare Tax. Additional Medicare tax for high earners is in addition to the 1.45% withheld on earned income up to the threshold. Add 0.9% Medicare tax on earned income at or above the threshold amount shown below.

If you owe this tax file Form 8959 with return. Any additional Medicare tax withheld by employer is also reported on this form. If normal pay is $200,000 or more employer must withhold the tax. If self-employed, include tax in estimated tax liability.

THRESHOLD AMOUNTS ARE:
Thresholds for 3.8% NII and 0.9% Medicare taxes are not indexed for inflation!!

Filing Status	Threshold Amount
Married filing jointly (MFJ)	$250,000
Married Filing separately	$125,000
Single	$200,000
Head of Households (w/qualifying person	$200,000
Qualifying Widow(er) w/dependent child	$250,000

6. Personal Exemption/Itemized Deductions Limits. The personal exemption ($4,050 for 2017) for all individuals and their dependents was REPEALED effective in 2018 (but may return after 2025). Also, for high income taxpayers the phaseout of itemized deductions limits, was TERMINATED in the new law.

7. Alternate Minimum Tax (AMT). The AMT was originally designed to make sure the wealthy paid some income tax. AMT works by not allowing certain deductions. An exemption amount exist so that many taxpayers are excluded from the AMT computations. The AMT exemption is subject to inflation and often changed by Congress.

NOTE: **The 1031 exchange deferred capital gain is not included in either normal income tax or added to AMT computations.**

8. Tax Forgiven Upon Death. Property is still received by heirs at Fair Market Value (FMV) - - and all the1031 exchange deferred gain and depreciation of the deceased owner are forgiven.

9. Estimated Tax Payments. If the property is SOLD the taxes described above will be due and should be paid. If you do not pay enough tax during the tax year you may have to pay a penalty.

10. Capital Gain Tax Worksheet. Starting in 2018 there was a major revision to basic Form 1040. Taxable Income, which includes the capital gain - is taxed at different rates. To determine the tax due on various types of income a form like the 'Schedule D Tax Worksheet' (see IRS Schedule D Instructions for a copy) must be completed. A similar worksheet should be published by the IRS for future year returns. This worksheet takes into consideration the different rates for the tax on capital gains of 0%,15% and 20%, Section 1250 depreciation recapture, the 28% rate, and tax on ordinary income at the normal bracket rate, but NOT the additional taxes. These are added, and the **TOTAL TAX DUE** is shown on the form 1040.

11. Application of 20% Capital Gain Rate.

Simple REC Rule: Only that portion of net capital gain taken from Line 16, Form 1040 that puts Taxable Income, over the top value dollar for the 15% capital gain bracket is taxed at 20%.

Example: If a taxpayer already has taxable income at the top of the 15% bracket and an additional $100,000 in long term capital profit and qualified dividends, the entire $100,000 would be subject to the 20% rate. If, however, the taxpayer has less than the top of the 15% bracket in taxable income and $100,000 in capital profit and qualified dividends, then only the additional amount above the top of the 15% bracket would be taxed at 20%.

12. No Interest or SALT Limitation on Business Property.

Taxpayers may continue to expense all interest and state and local taxes on business property (like residential rentals). Also, landlords are not required to pay Self-Employment taxes.

Below is a simple form that permits estimating of estimated basis and taxable gain if property is SOLD.

FIGURING ESTIMATED BASIS and TAXABLE GAIN

Knowing the current tax basis for a property is essential.

1. SELLING PRICE $_____
2. **Subtract** Selling Costs (use 8% of selling price if unknown)   - $_____
3. ADJUSTED SELLING PRICE $_____
4. Original Cost Basis $_____
5. **Add** Improvements   + $_____
6. EQUALS ADJUSTED COST BASIS   = $_____
7. **Subtract** All Depreciation Taken/ Authorized   - $_____
   (if unknown, take 3% of original cost X number of years owned)
8. TAX BASIS (**Subtract** line 7 from line 6)   = $_____
9. TAXABLE GAIN if property is sold
   (**subtract** line 8 from line 1)   = $_____

Remember additional taxes may be added as a result of the increased Taxable Gain being added to normal income

Chapter 5

REINVESTMENT REQUIREMENTS

1. **Total Deferral Of Capital Gains Tax.** One of the primary objectives of a §1031 tax deferred exchange is to defer paying any tax on the gain realized - the potential capital gain, including depreciation recapture.

For an exchange to be **totally tax free** in the year of sale the reinvestment in the replacement property or properties must meet all the following rules:

Rule 1 - Replacement property(ies) must have an equal or greater acquisition cost then the adjusted selling price of the relinquished property(ies).

Rule 2 - All the cash received from the transfer of the relinquished property must be reinvested.

Rule 3 - Replacement property should have a new or assumed mortgage total that is equal to or greater than the debt paid off on the relinquished property – **or the exchangor must add new cash to offset the difference.**

Rule 4 - Exchanger should not receive non-like property – including owner held notes, cash or personal property.

> **Warning** – To defer all gain, the new replacement property(ies) must be at least the adjusted selling price of the relinquished property(ies) –

> **NOT just reinvestment of the Capital Gain.**

2. **Depreciation Tax.** The capital gain deferred also includes the depreciation that has been taken on the property.

3. **Acquisition Cost.** The acquisition cost is the contract price plus the acquisition expenses which are part of the cost to acquire the property. Normally these are shown on the Settlement Statement. The acquisition expenses do not include prepaid items, such as real estate taxes and hazard insurance, or expenses associated with obtaining financing, such as points. IRS Publication 551 provides a list of costs that can be added to basis. If an expense can be added to basis it is also considered an 'exchange expense'

The cash in the qualified escrow account may be used toward both the down payment and acquisition expenses.

4. **Earnest Money Deposit.** In order to be tax-free the basic rules pertaining to an earnest money deposit are:

> (1) the taxpayer/exchangor **may not** receive directly from the Qualified Intermediary (QI) any of the cash being held in the qualified escrow account.

> (2) the taxpayer may use their own personal funds to make the earnest money deposit.

> (3) the QI may not use any of the escrow account funds toward purchase of the replacement property until all the rights of the taxpayer in the contract for the replacement property has been assigned to the QI.

> (4) cash paid to purchase the replacement property offsets cash received from the QI or settlement agent after settlement of the last replacement property.

The following conditions and examples will explain the process as it pertains to earnest money deposits.

> Situation: the taxpayer/exchanger agrees to purchase a replacement property for $400,000. The contract requires a $20,000 earnest money deposit. The QI has $300,000 from the transfer of the relinquished property in the escrow account.

> Example #1: the taxpayer writes a personal check for $20,000 for the earnest money at the time the contract for the replacement property is written. This is considered new cash. Prior to the closing the taxpayer decides to let it ride and not request reimbursement. The end effect is that the loan amount is less.

Example #2: after giving a personal check for the earnest money deposit the taxpayer decides that at closing they must receive the amount of the earnest deposit back. If all the other replacement values are met to purchase the replacement property the loan value will be reset to insure there is sufficient cash left over at closing. The settlement agent will return the earnest money deposit to the taxpayer.

Example #3: after the taxpayer writes a check for the earnest money deposit they decide they want their cash back. After the replacement property contract has been assigned by the taxpayer to the QI, the QI may write a check for the earnest money deposit using the funds in the qualified escrow account. This is normally given to the real estate brokerage or settlement firm. Then whomever is holding the taxpayers earnest money deposit funds, after receiving the substitute earnest money deposit check returns the funds to the taxpayer.

Example #4. if the taxpayer does not have or wish to write a personal check for the earnest money deposit they may include in the contract the provision that the QI will pay the earnest money deposit after the contract is approved by the seller and the contract has been assigned to the QI. When this has been accomplished the QI will then write an earnest money deposit check from the funds in the qualified escrow account.

5. **Partial Tax Deferred Exchange.** It is possible that the situation will arise when the Exchangor wants or ends up receiving **BOOT** — that is taxable income. There are three basic sources of boot. These are —

   a. **Cash Boot.** Cash proceeds received at settlement or at the end of the exchange process are taxable income up to the amount of the total realized gain. The investor needs $50,000 in cash immediately and receives it at settlement of the relinquished property from the settlement agent.

Sales Proceeds (Before Tax)	$370,000
Cash Received (Taxable Income)	50,000
Cash to be Reinvested	$320,000

   b. **Mortgage Boot.** Mortgage relief (the mortgages on the replacement properties are less then the total mortgages on the relinquished properties) also becomes BOOT and taxable income.

      IMPORTANT. However, new cash in — that is adding new cash to the down payment can offset mortgage Boot. Let us say for some reason the total new mortgage debt on the replacement properties is only $50,000

Total Current Mortgages	$90,000
Total New Mortgages	50,000
Mortgage Boot (Taxable)	$40,000

Remember!! New cash can offset Mortgage Boot

c. **Non-Like Property Boot.** If the exchanger were to receive non-like property in the transaction, say an automobile, it is considered as taxable income at market value. More common is when the exchanger takes back financing on the relinquished property. The value of the Note received is considered Boot and is taxable gain. With proper planning the Note will be treated as an installment sale and will be taxed as the gain is received over the term of the loan. The fact that the Note is sold at settlement by the exchanger does not change this situation. If at all possible, the exchanger should avoid taking back financing on the relinquished property.

6. Boot and the Reduced Price for the Replacement.
If the exchanger decides to 'buy down' — that is to purchase a replacement property that has an acquisition cost less then the adjusted sale price of the relinquished property we know immediately that the exchanger will have some taxable income.

If the adjusted sales price of the relinquished property was $460,00, and the exchanger purchased a replacement property that cost $410,00 we know there will be $50,000 of potential capital gain recognized. The exchanger can take all of the $50,000 in cash or can reduce the new mortgage amount.

For planning purposes, if you know in advance that the exchanger desires cash out from the transaction then you can reduce the target price for the replacement property.

For example: the exchanger wants $50,000 in cash at settlement of the relinquished property.

To be totally tax-free acquisition cost should be at least:	$460,000
Exchangor desires cash out of	−$ 50,000
For balance of capital gain of $305,000 to be deferred	
the replacement property should cost at least:	$ 410,000

Caution: To avoid taxable boot, rent and security deposit adjustments should be made outside of closing.

7. Size of Loan. To avoid cash boot Exchangers should be careful that the **size of the loan** on the replacement property isn't so high that they inadvertently receive **taxable cash boot** back at settlement. To defer all of the tax — the cash received from the transfer of the relinquished property must be used as **down payment** on the replacement property. The **loan amount** will then be the difference between the amount needed to purchase the property and the down payment. Be certain that the amount of your loan on the replacement property does not result in your getting cash at settlement in excess of your personal earnest money deposit.

> **Boot Offsetting Rule: Mortgage boot can be offset with new cash, — but cash boot cannot be offset with additional mortgage.**

8. Purchase of Partial Ownership. There are a number of situations that can occur in which the exchanger is only purchasing a percent interest in the replacement property. The 1031 exchange will still be valid and there will be deferral of the tax if the exchanger complies with the reinvestment rules set forth in the first part of this Chapter.

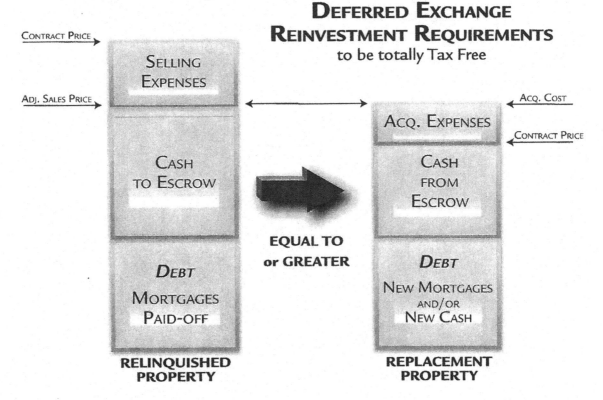

DEFERRED EXCHANGE REINVESTMENT REQUIREMENTS
to be totally Tax Free

21

Chapter 6

CRITICAL ELEMENTS

1. **Critical Elements.** There are some activities in the execution of a 1031 exchange that must be timely and properly accomplished. While these activities may be explained in other chapters they are grouped together in this chapter and called <u>critical elements</u>. These elements are often reviewed to make sure the 1031 exchange is valid and the gain can be deferred.

   The seven critical elements are: a) intent, b) form and documentation, c) control of funds, d) like-kind properties, e) time limits, f) continuity of title and disqualified person.

2. **Intent.**

   Declaring intent to do an to exchange is not a requirement. But exchangers should specify their intent to do an exchange. If there is ever a question about a transaction, courts have looked to the intent of the exchanger. There are several ways to declare intent.

   a. **Declare Intent in the Multiple Listing**
      Declare the intent to exchange in a multiple listing system. *We do not recommend reflecting that a seller is doing a 1031 exchange in a listing.* If a prospective buyer is unaware of what a 1031 exchange is and how it will not impact them, they may not want to look at the property listed.

   b. **Declare Intent in the Sale Contract**. Typically, a 1031 exchange addendum language added to a sale and purchase agreement will reflect intent to do an exchange, allow the assignment of the rights to the contract, ask for the other parties' cooperation and declare that the 1031 exchange will have no impact on the other party. There is no question that the assignment of the contract rights to the QI must occur in the exchange process. It is clear in the IRS Regulation 1.1031(k)-1(g)(4)(iv) and (v) *that "if the rights of a party to the agreement are assigned to the intermediary and all parties to that agreement are notified in writing of the assignment on or before the date of the relevant transfer of property"* the QI is treated as entering into the agreement. The assignment document and notification to all parties are normally provided by the QI.

A 1031 addendum will normally clearly show intent to do a 1031 exchange, permit assignment, and advise the other party there will be no expense or liability as a result of the exchange. Sometimes there is "cooperation" language asserting that both parties to the contract will cooperate with a 1031 exchange. Such an addendum may be necessary to overcome 'no assignment' language in some realtor contracts. However, concerns have been expressed over the need for such an addendum. These concerns are twofold. First, the other parties will not permit any assignment. Second, the exchanger may not want to disclose that the sale or purchase is a possible 1031 transaction for fear of jeopardizing his negotiating position and possibly the price. When an exchanger discloses that he is attempting to complete a 1031 exchange, he alerts the seller of the replacement property that the exchanger, as the buyer, has gain to be deferred from taxes, as well as a 1031 time frame to meet. Exchangers must be very careful that they do not give up a negotiating position.

There are cases where an exchanger decides to do an exchange at the very last-minute right before closing on the relinquished property. Thus, there is no time to amend the sale agreement to declare intent.

c.   **Declare Intent in the Exchange Agreement.** The Exchange Agreement between the Exchangers and Qualified Intermediary (QI) normally clearly states it is the intent of the Exchanger to exchange currently owned property for replacement property. *This is the ideal way to establish intent.*

In recent years, some Associations of Realtors® have incorporated language into their standard contract or addendum that the parties will cooperate and allow an assignment to complete a 1031 exchange.

While reflecting the intent to do a 1031 exchange in a listing or reflecting the intent in the sale contract in the overwhelming majority of cases will do no harm. However, an exchanger needs to be aware of the potential down side of disclosing the intent to do an exchange to the other party.

3. Control of Funds.

At no time in the 1031 exchange process can the Exchanger have any control or otherwise obtain any **benefits** from the cash held in the exchange escrow account. In a 1031 exchange, gain or loss may be recognized (become taxable income) if the exchangers actually or constructively receive money or other property before they actually receive all the like-kind replacement property. The exchangers are considered in actual receipt if they receive money or the economic benefit of the money or other property. They are in constructive receipt when the money is credited to their account or otherwise made available to them. The exchanger is not considered in receipt if substantial limitations or restrictions on receipt of the money or benefits exits. However, constructive receipt occurs when the limitations or restrictions lapse, expire or are waived. To put it in the simplest terms:

> # The Exchanger can have no control of the exchange escrow funds!!

In some states, like Virginia, where it is required by law that the exchange escrow funds be in a separately identified deposit account, that is a qualified escrow or qualified trust account in a financial institution. Any withdrawals require the written authorization of the exchanger. To help taxpayers avoid actual or constructive receipt exchangers may use the procedures or "safe harbors" established by the IRS in the regulation Section 1.1031(k)-1(g). A copy of the current IRC 1031 is in the Appendix.

One of the Safe Harbors is the use of a qualified escrow or trust account. A qualified escrow account exist when the account holder is not the exchanger or a disqualified person. And *"the **escrow agreement** expressly limits the taxpayer's rights to receive, pledge, borrow or otherwise obtain the benefits of the cash or cash equivalent held in the escrow account."* There are additional restrictions placed on disbursements from the exchange escrow account. These are known as the **(g)(6)** restrictions. In the event the exchanger does not identify replacement properties and wishes to terminate the exchange the holder of the escrow may not disburse any funds until the end of the 45 day identification period. Also if the exchanger properly identifies replacement properties then the escrow holder can only disburse funds if — **(a) the 180 day exchange period has passed, or (b)the exchangers have received all of the replacement property to which they are entitled under the agreement.**

Warning: There must be a specific written agreement between the exchanger and the party holding the escrow funds (normally the QI) that includes the above **(g)(6)** restrictions. Simply leaving the funds with the settlement attorney, title company or putting in a bank account, or giving the funds to another third party does not meet the requirements for the safe harbor. **It is critical the written agreement and assignment of contract be accomplished before settlement of the first relinquished property.**

4. **Form and Documentation.** To properly reflect the transaction as an exchange and not a sale, close compliance with the documentation requirements of the regulations is critical. In the '1031 Exchange Process' in Chapter 8 there is a review of each document that is essential to the exchange process. Also provided in the Appendix is a **checklist** to assist exchangers meet all the required exchange documentation. The necessary documents and the time line involved with a reverse exchange are also critical and are fully explained in Chapter 10.

Often at settlement of the property being sold the taxpayer will learn about doing a 1031 Exchange. With the electronic capability that exist today, a QI is able to prepare an Exchange Agreement and send it to the settlement office for signature of the taxpayer and return to the QI. **Remember the Exchange Agreement and assignment of contract must be signed before the settlement takes place or the transaction will be considered a sale and taxes will be due.**

5. **Like-Kind Properties.** To defer gain in a 1031 exchange, property held for productive use in a trade or business or for investment must be exchanged for property that will also be held as a business or investment.

For **real property** this is simple, 'real estate for real estate'. An apartment house can be exchanged for a farm, a warehouse for an office building, unimproved for improved real estate.

Over the years there have been efforts to change *like-kind* to *similar*. Meaning a residential rental house could only be exchanged for another residential rental house, etc. So far §1031 remains unchanged as like-kind,

6. **Time Limits.** The replacement exchange property(ies) must be identified within 45 days of settlement or transfer of the relinquished property and then settled or transferred within 180 days, which is called the **Exchange Period**. These are critical dates, and fully explained in Chapter 7, 'Identification and Exchange Period'. As a QI there are many calls from exchangers wishing to extend or manipulate the suspense dates or required documentation. Exchangers should clearly understand these are *suspense dates required by law that cannot be changed.* [dates can only be extended in a Presidential Declared Disaster] The period allowed are calendar days, with no weekend or holiday excusals.

7. **Continuity of Title.** While not specifically stated in IRC 1031 a basic rule when doing a like-kind exchange is that there must be continuity of title. This is often called the "same taxpayer rule". It means that title to the interest in the property being purchased, the replacement property, must be the same as the name of the party or entity holding title to the property being sold, the relinquished property. Of course with any rule there are exceptions. The three exceptions pertaining to the transfer and receipt of exchange property are 1) exchanger's revocable living trust, 2) exchanger's single member limited liability company (LLC), and 3) a Delaware Statutory Trust. These are all considered by the IRS as **disregarded entities**. In community property states, mostly in the West, a husband and wife two party LLC is allowed as a 'disregared entity'.

8. **Disqualified Person.** A disqualified person may not hold the escrow account, receive identification notice, or serve as a qualified intermediary. Basically, a disqualified person is an agent of the taxpayer at the time of the transaction. A person considered an agent is a) one who has acted as the taxpayer's employee, attorney, accountant, investment broker, or real estate agent or broker within the two-year period ending on the date of transfer of the first relinquished property, b) is a family member and related parties. This includes brothers and sisters, half-brothers and sisters, spouse, ancestors (parents, grandparents, etc.), and lineal descendants (children, grandchildren, etc.). In-laws are not included. A related party also includes corporations, partnerships, and trusts in which the exchanger or a disqualified party have a greater than 10% interest. If the person and the exchanger, and/or the person and the exchanger's agent "bear a relationship described in either section 267(b) or section 707(b), then 10% is substituted in each section for '50 %' each place it appears."

Note: Not considered an agent is a person who performs exchange services, like a QI, or a financial institute, or title company that provides routine financial, title insurance, escrow or trust services.

Warning: If a totally independent person is not being utilized to ensure proper control of the escrow funds, serve as Qualified Intermediary, or to receive identification notice, the exchanger should seek legal review of Section 1.1031(k)-1(k) to be certain a "disqualified person" is not involved.

Chapter 7

IDENTIFICATION AND EXCHANGE PERIODS

1. Time Limits. IRC Section 1031(a)(3)still clearly provides two time limits which are very important and require strict compliance. These are:

a. The replacement property or properties to be acquired in the exchange <u>must be identified</u> before the end of the <u>identification period.</u>

"The identification period begins on the date the taxpayer transfers the relinquished property and ends at midnight on the 45th day thereafter."

b. The identified replacement property <u>must be received</u> by the end of the <u>exchange period.</u>

"The exchange period begins on the date the taxpayer transfers the relinquished property and ends at midnight on the **earlier** of the 180th day thereafter **or** the **due date** (including extensions) for the taxpayer's return"

The time starts for both the **identification and exchange periods** when the first property being relinquished is transferred.

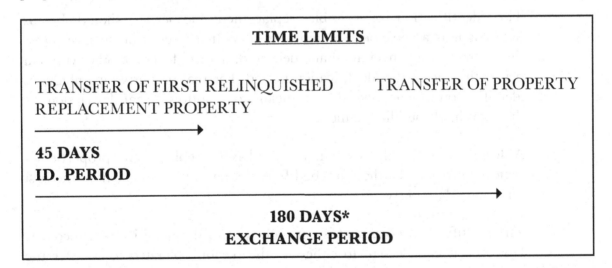

*The earlier of 180 days or the due date (including on time extensions) of tax return for tax year when transfer of first relinquished property occurs.

NOTE: The total exchange period is 180 days. This includes the 45 day ID period. So, if an exchanger uses 45 days to ID replacement property, the period remaining until the end of the exchange period is only 135 days.

2. On Time Extension.

The replacement property must be settled within 180 days **OR** the tax return due date, whichever is earlier. If the exchange property being relinquished settles late in the year then it may be necessary for exchangers to file IRS Form 4868 <u>on-time</u> to get an automatic extension to October 15th.

Example: the relinquished property settles on December 15, 2020 and the tax return for 2020 is due on April 15, 2021. This would **not** give the exchanger the full 180 days to get to settlement on the replacement property. By filing an **on-time** extension the exchanger could then get the full 180 days from settlement of the relinquished property to complete the exchange.

3. Extension For Presidentially Declared Disasters.

The only allowed extension of the 45-day, 180 day, or 'reverse exchange' time limits occurs if some element of the exchange is covered under a Presidentially Declared Disaster or the exchanger is in a combat zone. (For details see Chapter 14)

4. Identification Rules.

While no specific rules were set forth in the Tax Reform Act of 1984, which established the requirement, as to how the identification was to be made, the IRS regulations published in 1991 provide specific guidance on how to identify replacement properties.

    a.   The identification of possible replacement properties should be as unambiguous as possible, contained in a written document or agreement, signed by the exchanger and hand delivered, mailed, faxed, or otherwise sent before the end of the identification period. For real property, unambiguous identification is generally taken to mean street address, legal description, or distinguishable building name.

            A form letter for the exchanger to identify replacement properties is typically provided by the Qualified Intermediary after settlement of the first relinquished property.

            The identification document is normally sent to the qualified intermediary. However, it can be sent to either — the person obligated to transfer the replacement property to the exchanger, or any other person involved in the exchange other than the exchanger or a disqualified person. The written identification may be a separate document or contained in the actual contract/agreement for the replacement property.

Important: Any replacement property actually received before the end of the identification period will be considered as identified. But it must be counted in later 3 property or 200% identifications.

b.   The exchanger may identify more than one replacement property. However, regardless of the number of relinquished properties transferred by the exchanger as part of the same deferred exchange, the maximum number of replacement properties that may be identified is:

1)   **three** properties of any fair market value (FMV), **OR**
2)   any number of properties provided fair market value of identified properties, at end of identification period, does not exceed **200%** of fair market value of all relinquished properties.

c.   Identification may be **revoked** in writing anytime during the 45-day identification period and new properties identified.

d.   If at the end of the identification period, the taxpayer has identified more properties than permitted, the taxpayer will be treated as if no replacement property has been identified. Exception: Any replacement property received before the end of the identification period will be considered identified. Only if, properties properly identified and received before the end of the exchange period equal to at least 95% of all identified properties.

e.   Incidental property is disregarded in the identification if in a normal commercial transaction it is typically transferred with the larger property (example-washers and dryers) and the aggregate fair market value of the incidental property does not exceed 15% of the FMV of the larger property.

Important: When after the identification is made the replacement property will be constructed or improved, OR the exchanger will be only purchasing a partial interest in the replacement property the following special identification rules apply.

5.   Identification of Property to be Built. The regulations provide special rules for the identification and receipt of replacement property to be built. These special rules apply when identification of a replacement property is made – and **before receipt of the property** – it will be in whole or part constructed, built, installed, manufactured, developed or improved. The identification requirement for the property to be built will be met if the identification provides "a legal description for the underlying land and as much detail is provided regarding construction of the improvements as is practicable at the time the identification is made.

6. Separate Properties. The IRS normally will not treat noncontiguous properties or separate adjacent lots as a single property. Each property will count in the 3 property or 200% rules.

7. Identification of a Partial Interest. When an exchanger plans to purchase a partial interest in a replacement property, the 45 day identification must show the share to be purchased by the exchanger (example: a 40% interest in 123 Baker Street, Any Town, NC). The exchanger should make certain the percentage share on the ID and the deed or on the settlement statement are the same.

Important: Improvements to be made to property already OWNED by the exchanger are **not** considered like-kind.

Example: A like kind exchange cannot be used to build a house on a lot already owned.

8. When Does the Transfer or Receipt of Property Occur? The beginning of the 45 day identification period and the 180 day exchange period are both triggered by the "transfer" of the first relinquished property. For Federal income tax purposes ownership of real property occurs upon the transfer of the "benefits and burdens" of ownership.

> *The following are several factors that are considered in determining if ownership has transferred.(1) whether legal title passed; (2) how the parties treat the transaction; (3) whether an equity was acquired in the property; (4) whether the contract creates a present obligation on the seller to execute and deliver a deed and a present obligation on the purchaser to make payments; (5) whether the right of possession is vested in the purchaser; (6) which party pays the property taxes; (7) which party bears the risk of loss or damage to the property; and (8) which party receives the profits from the operation and sale of the property. [From "Tax-Free Exchanges Under Section 1031", by Mary Foster.]*

Most often we use the settlement date on the Settlement Statement as the "transfer" date. Unfortunately, this date is often earlier than the actual transfer date due to a last minute delay in settlement. Exchangers should always check their settlement statement and their 45 and 180 day suspense dates to be sure they reflect the proper "transfer" date.

9. Identification Option. Some QI identification letter formats provide an option for the exchanger to declare they will only acquire only one or more of the three properties they have identified. Thus, some exchangers use this option when they use the three property rule to do their 45 day identification letter. Stating they only intend to acquire one or a specific number of the identified properties. To date the IRS has not specifically rule on the use of such options in the 45 day identification letter.

Chapter 8

1031 EXCHANGE PROCESS

1. **Deferred Exchange.** Today almost all exchanges are deferred exchanges. That is, there is a delay between the settlement of the relinquished property and the replacement property. Such exhanges are conducted following the provisions of IRS regulation section 1.1031 (k) -1 (see copy in Appendix).

For the investor, business man, and real estate broker/agent the regulations provide a simple process which fits nicely with normal day to day real estate operations. This process permits the normal real estate listing and purchase contract process to work for all parties involved. It provides time to sell the exchanger's property, to locate and place under contract new property(ies) and go to settlement in an orderly fashion. By using a QI the exchanger is not dependent on the buyer or seller agreeing to be involved in the process.

2. **Use of Qualified Intermediary.** For the 'Safe Harbor' provisions of the regulations to apply an exchanger must use a QI in a tax-deferred exchange. IRS defines a QI as:

    > "a person who is not the taxpayer or a disqualified person, and enters into a written agreement with the taxpayer and as required by the exchange agreement, acquires the relinquished property from the taxpayer, transfers the relinquished property, acquires the replacement property, and transfers the replacement property to the taxpayer".

3. **The Exchange Process.** The process starts with the listing of the property being relinquished. After the exchanger has a contract on the relinquished property and provides a copy to the QI – which is most often a corporation set-up specifically to do exchanges – to prepare the exchange and escrow account agreement which outlines each step in the exchange process. Normally the exchange agreement is prepared and signed **after** there is a ratified contract on the property to be relinquished. (See chart on next page showing the full process).

Prior to settlement the QI must be assigned the purchase contract for the relinquished property. All parties to the contract are notified of the assignment on or before settlement.

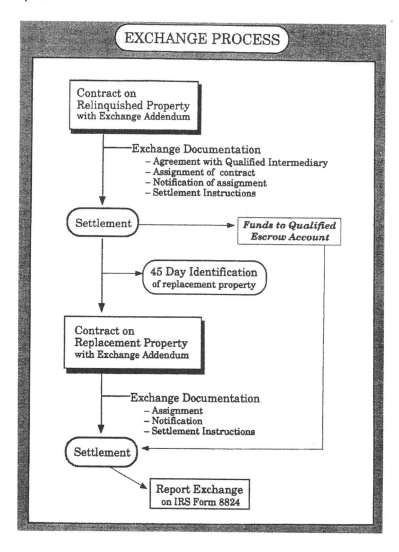

Important. The agreement and the assignment must be signed, and the Notification of Assignment made prior to settlement of the first relinquished property.

At settlement, the property being relinquished is transferred from the exchanger to the QI. Immediately the QI transfers the property to the buyer. The funds from the buyer are placed in a qualified escrow account (Virginia law requires they be in a financial institution for VA based QIs or Virginia property.) so that the exchanger has no control over them.

Note: Title will be conveyed directly from the owner/exchanger to the purchaser as authorized by Revenue Ruling 90-34.

The QI remains an important player in the exchange. The replacement property(ies) must be identified by the exchanger within 45 days. Any contracts are assigned to the QI and all parties to the contract are notified. At settlement the QI provides the funds from the escrow account, receives the replacement property and transfers it to the exchanger.

As soon as legally possible, the QI will disburse all remaining funds, provide a final accounting and forward any interest. The role of the QI is then complete.

4. **Advance Preparation of Exchange Documentation.** The most desirable method for handling exchange documentation is to have it completed and signed prior to settlement. Some of the many advantages to having documents signed in advance are:

   o The exchanger/seller is confident that all required documents for the exchange to take place have been completed. Too often a seller will show up at settlement thinking an exchange will take place and nothing has been done in advance.
   o No additional action is required at closing by the settlement agent/attorney. No documents pertaining to the exchange need to be signed.
   o The QI can answer any questions the exchanger has about the exchange in advance of settlement. Normally the settlement agent/attorney is not willing or is not qualified to answer questions at the settlement table.

There is less confusion and stress at settlement for both the buyer and seller when all exchange documents have been signed in advance.

5. **Early Replacement Property Contract.** A replacement property contract may be written before the relinquished property is listed or under contract – but the replacement property may **not** go to settlement early.

Chapter 9

RELATED PERSONS

1. **Introduction**. An exchange may be made with a related person, however IRC § 1031(f) imposes restrictions on such exchanges. Related person exchanges have generated a great number of questions from exchangers, many rulings from the IRS, and a large number of discussions within the QI industry. In the following paragraphs we will cover the basic rules, the reasons for these rules, who is a related person, and the most important IRS rulings that provide guidance for related person exchanges. Unfortunately, there have been many Private Letter Rulings (PLR) issued by the IRS, which apply only to the exchange under review, and may not be used as a precedent, and do not cover all exchanges as would be covered in a Revenue Ruling or Revenue Procedure. So the PLRs provide most of the guidance followed in related person exchanges. All PLRs are not positive, taxpayers should be aware that some rulings disallow the exchange tax deferral.

2. **Basic Law.** IRC § 1031, subsection (f)(4), was added to IRC § 1031 in 1989 to deny non-recognition of the capital gain if either the related person in an exchange or the exchanger dispose of the property received within two years of the date of the last transfer which was part of the exchange. Also, the IRS published Revenue Ruling 2002-83 on November 26, 2002 to address the applicability of IRS§1031(f)(4) to the purchase by an exchanger of a replacement property from a related person using a QI.

Revenue Ruling 2002-83 makes it clear that the use of a QI in a transaction with a related person does not make it a non-related person exchange and the § 1031(f)(4) rulings still apply.

3. **Reason for the Law.** Before the law was amended in 1989 it was legal for related parties to do an exchange. However, there was a great deal of concern that in exchanges between related parties there was a basis shift between properties before the relinquished property was sold by the new related owner. This is best explained by the following example.

Example: A father has owned an apartment house for a number of years. He paid $250,000 for the property new, and now he can sell it for $750,000. He has taken depreciation over the years and now has an adjusted basis of $125,000 in the property. His son had bought an overpriced shopping center for $1 million but it didn't do well and is now worth $750,000. The sons' shopping center is a great investment at $750,000. The father really likes the shopping center at $750,000 but if he sells his apartment house to buy from his son he'll have a huge taxable gain. Between father and son they decide to simultaneously exchange properties, they swap deeds. In an exchange the existing basis carries forward to the new property. The father now has carried forward his basis into the son's investment property. Dad's new basis in the shopping center is $125,000 and all the gain is deferred. The son's basis in the apartment house is $1,000,000. The basis have been shifted. The son now sells the apartment house for $750,000 and recognizes the loss of $250,000 and pays no tax on the sale. Among the family they were able to keep the shopping center, without dad having to pay taxes and son was able to trigger his loss. The related parties now have $750,000 cash, the father has a new property worth $750,000 and Uncle Sam collected no capital gain tax.

It is clear that the related parties can still do a 'direct exchange' if both properties received are held for two years. Even if a sale is contemplated after the two years. A 'direct exchange' occurs when the parties swap properties directly with each other. This normally occurs simultaneously and may involve a qualified intermediary. However, regardless of the time the exchanger holds the new replacement property, or the use of a QI, it is clear that purchase of the replacement property from a related person may result in the IRS questioning and disallowing the exchange.

4. **Exceptions.** Over the years there have been rulings which clarify exceptions to the basic rule. An important exception is if the related person seller of the replacement property is not cashing out (that is, they are also doing an exchange), then the replacement property may be purchased from a related person. A taxpayer or related party can receive some boot without causing the entire exchange to fail and be taxable.

5. **What Is The Two Year Period?** The IRC § 1031 law is clear that if a taxpayer truly exchanges property with a related person there is a recognition of gain if the taxpayer or related person disposes of the property received "before the date two years after the date of the last transfer which was part of such exchange". The law provides certain exceptions to the two year rule in subsection (f)(2). A person may plan to sell the property after the two year period passes. Fortunately, any gain recognized in a failed exchange shall be reported as of the date on which the disposition occurs. This eliminates the need for submission of amended tax returns. Unfortunately, any loss cannot be initially claimed but is an adjustment to the basis. (§ 267(a)(1).

Example: Taxpayer transfers relinquished property to related person on March 10, 2014 and takes title to the replacement property five months later on August 10, 2014. The two year period for both parties starts on August 10, 2014.

6. **Definition Of A Related Person.** A "related person" means any person bearing a relationship to the exchanger as set forth in IRC § 267(b) or § 707(b)(1) and explained in IRS Publication 544. For example under these rules related parties include you and a member of your family (spouse, brother, sister, parent, child, etc.); you and a corporation in which you have more than 50% ownership; and you and a partnership/ LLC in which you own more than a 50% interest. Note that an in-law, aunt, uncle, cousin, nephew, niece or ex-spouse may be a relative in your family, but are not a related "person" by definition.

    You should consult with your tax advisor if there is any doubt as to the related person status of the seller of the replacement property.

When reporting the exchange be **certain** that the other party in the exchange is a related person as explained in this chapter (For instance, an in-law while a relative, is not a related person). Also be certain the exchange is a related party exchange (For example, if the related property owner of the replacement property did not cash out and also did an exchange, it would not be reported as a related party exchange).

If you decide it is a related person exchange you are required to file for the two years following the year Form 8824 is first filed. See Form 8824 and its instructions.

7. **Avoiding Related Person Status.** Since any transaction between related parties may be called into question by the IRS it is better to avoid the other person being a related person by taking action early to transfer ownership of the property to a non-related party. For example, if you own an investment property, and want to buy your sisters property and she is cashing out, buying from your sister would be a related party transaction.

If your sister were to transfer her share of a property to her husband, now the husband has 100% ownership, your exchange would be your purchasing 100% from a in-law which is not a related party transaction. If you are a trustee of a trust in which your niece is a beneficiary, you may resign as a trustee in advance, so that your niece is not a related person. The unrelated party should hold the interest and not transfer it back to the related party. Avoidance of a step or sham transaction, or an agreement for the related party to reacquire the property is a concern and should be avoided.

The IRS in many private letter rulings has found that related persons who exchange or swap interest are not trying for tax avoidance and therefore the transaction can be an exception to the related person rules. Usually, the transaction, as a result of an inheritance, involves the exchange of undivided interests in different properties that results in each related person holding a 100% interest in one of the properties or a larger undivided interest in one of the properties.

8. Sale Of Relinquished Property To Related Person. If you sell a property you own to a person who may be a related person by definition, and you purchase your replacement property from a **non-related** person, you are not performing a related person exchange as covered by § 1031(f)(4). In other words, the related person rules are not applicable if you are only selling to a related person, and then as part of the exchange buying the replacement property from a non-related third party. This transaction does not require Part 2 of the Form 8824 to be completed.

There are a number of real world situations in which the taxpayer may want to sell the relinquished property to a related person. For instance, if the taxpayer is considering the land owned being developed into lots and sold, but is afraid capital gain in the property will convert to ordinary income because of dealer activities. Another example, is a reverse exchange, a related person may purchase the relinquished property, if the exchange accommodation titleholder (EAT) has taken title to the replacement property. Thus allowing the taxpayer to successfully complete the exchange with the QI, and the reverse exchange with the EAT within the required 180 day period. This is particularly useful if the taxpayer cannot find another person in time to buy the relinquished property before the replacement property must settle. The IRS in a PLR has made the determination that a true sale of the relinquished property to a related person does not cause application of § 1031(f)(4) because the related person did not own prior to the exchange any property that the taxpayer acquired in the exchange. Because an exchange with a related person does not occur, the two year restriction in § 1031(f) does not apply and the related person is not required to hold the relinquished property purchased for two years. This is important if the related person continues to try and market the property, as there is no longer any 180 day restriction. When we use the term "true sale", we mean that the purchase price of the relinquished property should be FMV supported by an appraisal. The sale may be for cash, or a third party mortgage.

9. SUMMARY. While many issues with related person exchanges have been clarified by the IRS in private letter rulings, etc., over the past couple of years. There are sure to be a number of questions as exchange situations arise.

In summary, it can be stated that:

a. An exchanger can do a related person 'direct exchange'. A direct exchange occurs when the parties swap properties directly with each other. This normally occurs simultaneously and may involve a qualified intermediary. Both properties must be held for two years.

b. A related person can purchase the relinquished property. This is normally the start of a deferred exchange for the taxpayer using a QI, with the exchanger buying the replacement property from an unrelated party.

c. The IRS may disallow the exchange **if the replacement property is purchased from a related person**. This may occur regardless of the use of a QI, or how long the taxpayer holds the new replacement property. The exception to this restriction is that the related person is not "cashing out", but doing another exchange, even if some boot is going to be received. The requirement remains that the replacement property for both parties must be held for a period of two years.

d. Some related parties, such as in-laws, are not by definition related persons. Related person status can be avoided if transfer of ownership occurs well in advance of the exchange.

e. If a related exchange actually occurs, Part II of Form 8824 must be filed for the year of the transfer of the relinquished property, and for an additional two years.

Note: Related persons can swap undivided interest.

Chapter 10

REVERSE EXCHANGES

1. Reverse Exchange Background.

There are times when an investor or business exchanger wants or needs to get control of a desired replacement property before they can sell and transfer the relinquished property.

The exchange industry had for a number of years requested that the IRS establish some type of procedure to accommodate this situation. In the absence of IRS guidance exchangers were using third parties to take title to the eventual replacement property, having them own and operate the property, sometimes building improvements, until such time as the exchangor could transfer their relinquished property and purchase the replacement property from the third party owner. These are called "parking arrangements".

By definition §1031 only allows a forward exchange. A taxpayer must first give up their relinquished property and then take title to the replacement property.

The accommodating party (called an EAT) is either causing the transfer of the relinquished i.e. starting the exchange – or the accommodating party (EAT) will buy and hold the replacement title waiting for the sale of the relinquished property by the exchanger.

2. IRS Revenue Procedure 2000-37.
In September 2000 the IRS published IRS Revenue Procedure 2000-37 (A copy is in Appendix). This Procedure establishes "safe harbor" rules to formally provide for and document such "parking arrangements". The procedure requires that the eventual replacement property be held by the "exchange accommodation titleholder" (EAT) in accordance with a "qualified exchange accommodation arrangement" (QEAA). The written QEAA between the taxpayer and EAT must meet the following requirements:

1) The exchange accommodation titleholder (EAT) will have legal title to the property or "such other indicia of ownership".
2) It is the bona fide intent of the taxpayer to do an exchange.

43

A written Qualified Exchange Accommodation Agreement (QEAA) is prepared within five business days of transfer of ownership to the exchange accommodation titleholder (*It is strongly suggested the QEAA be written and signed before any property is transferred*), and the written agreement provides that:

1) the exchange accommodation titleholder is holding the property for the benefit of the taxpayer in order to complete an exchange under §1031;
2) the EAT will be treated as the beneficial owner of the property for federal income tax purposes; and
3) the EAT will file federal tax returns as necessary.

Within 45 days after transfer of ownership of the eventual replacement property to the EAT the r**elinquished property(ies)** to be exchanged must be identified. The taxpayer may identify alternate or multiple relinquished property as provided in §1.1031(k)-1(c)(4). This allows the exchanger to identify alternate property if the exchanger is uncertain which property(ies) will be finally included in the exchange.

No later than 180 days after transfer of ownership to the exchange accommodation titleholder, the replacement property must be transferred to the taxpayer.

3. Basic 1031 Exchange Required. When a taxpayer is going to do a reverse exchange, they often do not realize that a standard 1031 exchange using a QI must also occur.

CRITICAL. Following the basic 1031 exchange rules the taxpayer owned <u>relinquished</u> property must be transferred (sold) to a new owner before the taxpayer takes title to the replacement property. If the taxpayer takes title to the replacement property before the relinquished property is transferred the taxpayer may not do a 1031 exchange. **The exchanger cannot own both properties at the same time.**

A basic 1031 exchange with a QI must occur before the exchanger takes title to the replacement property. As later explained the EAT can take either the relinquished **OR** replacement property.

4. Exchange Accommodation Titleholder (EAT). Some Qualified Intermediary companies have set up separate entities or have made separate working arrangements with companies that have been established to serve as an exchange accommodation titleholder. Investors and business exchangers should use an experienced professional organization that is qualified to serve as a EAT.

The EAT may not be the taxpayer or a disqualified party as set forth in IRS Regulation 1.1031(k)-1(k). The EAT is disqualified if it is a related party or someone who has served as the investor's agent over the past two years. This includes the investor's attorney, real estate broker, employee or accountant.

5. Reverse Exchange Agreement (QEAA). The following legal or contractual arrangements are permitted and may be made without invalidating the Qualified Exchange Accommodation Arrangement (QEAA):

a. The taxpayer or a disqualified person may guarantee the obligations of the exchange accommodation titleholder, including debt, or may indemnify the exchange accommodation titleholder against cost and expenses.

b. The taxpayer or disqualified person may loan or advance funds to the exchange accommodation titleholder, or guarantee a loan or advance to the exchange accommodation titleholder.

c. The taxpayer or disqualified person may lease the property from the EAT.

d. The taxpayer or a disqualified person may manage the property, supervise improvement of the property, act as a contractor, or otherwise provide services to the exchange accommodation titleholder with respect to the property.

e. The taxpayer and exchange accommodation titleholder may enter into a contract relating to the purchase or sale of the property.

f. The exchange accommodation titleholder may also serve as the Qualified Intermediary.

6. How Does the Process Work. The EAT may take title to either the **replacement** property or the **relinquished** property.

If replacement Property.

The process for the EAT to take title to the eventual replacement property is basically as follows:

a. The taxpayer selects a QI to do the basic 1031 exchange part of the transaction.

b. Taxpayer ratifies the contract with the current owner to purchase replacement property.

c. Taxpayer selects an EAT to purchase and hold replacement property. Normally the EAT will be an LLC set up specifically for this transaction.

d. Taxpayer assigns replacement property contract to the EAT.

e. Taxpayer and EAT sign the Qualified Exchange Accommodation Arrangement (QEAA). This agreement also serves as the contract for taxpayer to purchase replacement property from EAT. There may also be Management and Lease agreements between the taxpayer and EAT. This gives the taxpayer the authority to manage the replacement property on a day-to-day basis, and to coordinate directly with any contractors.

f.   Taxpayer arranges for **financing** for EAT to purchase replacement property (usually a combination of a loan from the taxpayer to the EAT and the guarantee of a loan to the EAT by a commercial lender).

g.   EAT takes title to the replacement property.

h.   Taxpayer identifies relinquished property within 45 days of transfer of replacement property to EAT.

i.   Taxpayer receives contract on relinquished property, and completes normal exchange and escrow agreement along with assignment documentation with QI.

j.   Taxpayer/exchanger completes settlement on relinquished property. As necessary, the exchange escrow funds go to the qualified escrow account.

k.   As necessary, the taxpayer makes normal 45 day identification of replacement property.

l.   Taxpayer assigns QEAA (which includes contract to purchase replacement property) to QI. The QI then completes normal exchange documentation for replacement property.

m.   The replacement property is transferred directly from the EAT to the taxpayer/exchanger. The property is purchased with the exchange escrow funds from the QI, with the assumption of the loans made to the EAT or through new financing.

n.   Any additional exchange funds from the relinquished property sale are used to pay down the loan on the replacement property.

o.   Depending on the situation, in many cases, immediately after the closing of the relinquished property, the settlement of the replacement property being held by the EAT takes place. Transfer may be delayed for example if the replacement property is in a different state or new construction must be completed to meet the reinvestment requirements.

p.   Exchanger reports the exchange to the IRS on Form 8824 for the tax year relinquished property was sold. The EAT reports the transaction to the IRS and State tax authorities.

If Relinquished Property. Often, due to financing requirements on the replacement property, it is better for the EAT to take title to the relinquished property. This then sets up a normal exchange in which the taxpayer is transferring the relinquished property to the EAT before receiving the replacement property. To purchase the replacement property the exchanger must use his own funds and/or arrange new financing. The relinquished property must be transferred to the EAT before the replacement property is transferred to the taxpayer.

7. **Amendment of Rev. Proc 2000-37.** IRS Revenue Procedure 2004-51 modified Rev. Proc. 2000-37 to **not** allow a reverse exchange if taxpayer owned the replacement property in past 180 days.

8. **Non-Safe Harbor Parking.** It is possible to go beyond 180 days that a third party holds the eventual replacement property, but the safe harbor provisions will expire and the IRS may review the exchange.

Chapter 11

BASIS –DEPRECIATION –RECAPTURE

1. **Importance of Basis.** The importance of the tax basis of property cannot be over emphasized. In an exchange both the adjusted basis for the relinquished property and the new basis of the replacement property are easily figured but very important. The adjusted basis amount less any Exchange expenses will determine the Realized Gain that can be deferred in a 1031 exchange.

2. **Definition of Basis.** "Basis is the amount of your investment for tax purposes." This basis definition is from IRS Publication 551, Basis of Assets, which tells us of the many rules pertaining to the basis of different types of property. We will concentrate on figuring the basis for both the relinquished and replacement properties in a 1031 exchange.

3. **Adjusted Basis.** To figure the **Adjusted Basis** of the relinquished property we simply take the starting cost of the property, add improvements we have made, or other additions, and then subtract any depreciation taken or allowed.

4. **Different Starting Basis.** Each property may have a different starting basis, depending on how it was obtained by the current owners. We need to determine the correct starting basis before making adjustments over time and coming up with the current adjustable basis. The major different types of starting basis that exist are:

   a. **Normal Purchase**. Most investors start off with a normal purchase in which the basis for the property is the purchase price plus the expenses connected with the purchase. IRS Publication 551, list in part the following as normal expenses associated the purchase of a real property. These settlement expenses are added to your staring basis.
   1) abstract or title fee
   2) Charges for installing utility services
   3) legal fees
   4) recording fees
   5) surveys
   6) transfer taxes
   7) owner's title insurance
   8) amounts owed by seller that buyer agrees to pay, such as back taxes.

It important to note that the following are not settlement expenses and may **not** be added to the basis of real property.

1) fire insurance premiums
2) rent for occupancy before closing
3) charges for utility or other services related to occupancy before closing
4) charges connected with getting a loan, such as points, cost of a credit report, appraisal fees required by lender, mortgage insurance premiums, and loan assumption fees. Loan costs are amortized over the life of the loan and not added to the basis for the property. If the property is sold in later years all the unused loan costs not deducted may be claimed in the year of sale.

b. **Gifts and Inheritance of Real Property.** If the property was received as a gift your starting basis is the donor's adjusted basis at the time of the gift plus any gift tax paid on it. When a property is inherited, your basis is generally the fair market value (FMV) on the date of the individual's death.

c. **Joint ownership**. if you jointly own a property then your basis will be changed on the death of your co-owner. The new basis will be your adjusted basis plus the current FMV of the joint co-owner's interest on the date of death.

d. **Community Property.** In the community states of AZ., CA., Idaho, LA.,NV.,NM., TX., WA., and WI. when a spouse dies, the total value of the community property, even the part belonging to the surviving spouse, generally becomes the basis of the entire property.

e. **Like Kind Exchange.** Many investment properties have been purchased as part of a 1031 exchange. For an investment or business property obtained in an exchange after 1990 determining the starting basis is simple. For the tax year that the relinquished property was sold you filed with your Federal tax return IRS Form 8824. The last line on that form, Line 25, shows the total starting basis for your replacement property or properties. That starting basis was computed simply by taking the acquisition cost for the new replacement property less the gain deferred. If more than one replacement property is purchased then a starting basis is assigned to each property based on the ratio of the property's FMV to the total acquisition cost for the replacement properties.

In computing the new total basis for the replacement property IRS Publication 551 directs the Exchange Expenses be added to the basis of the replacement property.

5. What is Depreciation?

A property will decrease in value (not necessarily price) over time due to wear and tear, deterioration and age. Depreciation of such a property used in business or for investment, including rental, supposedly offsets the loss of value. A property used personally, such as your principal residence is never depreciated. Nor is land ever depreciated, although improvements made to

50

the land can be depreciated. If in doubt as to what percentage of property value is considered land, a taxpayer can look at the percentage created in the local property tax bill. Depreciation is considered a noncash expense. Thus, it will reduce the annual income reported on a property. However, the depreciation taken or allowed is recaptured if the property is sold. An advantage of a 1031 exchange is that the depreciation recapture tax can also be deferred.

6. **Current History of Depreciation.** There is little argument that depreciation has been the most changing area of real estate investing over the years. Depreciation was started in 1913 with the start of the income tax. It has been frequently used by the government to achieve social and financial objectives. While different depreciation methods were changed over the years, the period of history we are most concerned with began in 1981. In that year, President Regan and Congress passed the Economic Recovery Tax Act of 1981which created the Accelerated Cost Recovery System (ACRS). For rental real estate, property placed in service in 1981 was depreciated on a 175 percent declining balance formula with a 15 year recovery period. The ACRS also ignored salvage value and allowed taxpayers to depreciate the entire starting basis of the property. The ACRS allowances were liberal and truly did not reflect the economic loss in the value of assets due to wear and tear and obsolescence. The ACRS was a major factor in the increase of investor real estate activity and helped in the early recession of the eighties. In the 1984 Deficit Reduction Act the recovery period for real property was increased to 18 years. Then effective May 8, 1985 this was changed to 19 years. The Tax Reform Act of 1986 created the Modified ACRS or MACRS. The law created real property (real estate) depreciation recovery periods of 27.5 years for residential rental property and currently 39.0 years for nonresidential real property Also, real property is depreciated using the straight-line method using the midmonth convention. This stricter change in the method of depreciation along with reducing the assumption of loans, greatly reduced investor involvement in residential sales.

7. **Current Depreciation Rules.** Since depreciation rules are changed frequently by Congress, taxpayers are always encouraged to work with their accounting professionals to be certain current rules are being followed and all tax advantages are claimed.

8. **Depreciation Incorrectly Taken.** One of the comments we hear often from residential rental real estate sellers about to start an exchange with a relinquished property is that they have never taken depreciation. The basic principle is that whether you take depreciation or not, the IRS authorized depreciation and will always tax as if the depreciation was taken. When IRS allows a property to be depreciated, taxpayers should claim that depreciation on their tax return. The IRS will consider authorized depreciation as having been taken even if the taxpayer does not claim it. When a Section 1250 property (rental real estate) is sold,

the depreciation, taken or not, must be recaptured and is taxed at 25% (called 'Unrecaptured Section1250 Gain'). In an exchange, the tax on the gain is deferred.

When reporting the sale of or computing the gain or loss on rental property, you are required to make an adjustment to your basis for allowable depreciation regardless of whether the deduction was taken. For more information refer to IRS Publication 544, *Sales or Other Dispositions of Assets* and IRS Publication 946, *How to Depreciate Property*. If you neglected to take depreciation in the past, you can catch up and take the depreciation missed. This can be accomplished either by amended returns or filing long IRS Form 3335 based on when you placed the property in service. The details are contained in Pub 946.

9. Depreciation of 1031 Replacement Property.

In 2007 the IRS in T. D. published a regulation for depreciation of replacement property. Under this regulation, the general rule remains that the taxpayer must depreciate the remaining relinquished property adjusted basis (called the exchanged basis) over the remaining recovery period using the same depreciation method as if it were a continuation of the relinquished property depreciation schedule. However, if the replacement property is not residential, then the remaining exchanged basis and the new 'excess basis' would be depreciated using the 39 year schedule. Any increase in the basis (called the *excess basis*) will be treated as newly acquired property and will be depreciated over 27.5 or 39 years using a new straight-line depreciation schedule. No depreciation is claimed for the period between the transfer of the relinquished property and the receipt of the replacement property. The regulation does permit the taxpayer to elect-out of the rules and to treat the entire replacement property as a new asset.

Example: An exchanger has been taking depreciation for 10 years on a residential rental purchased for $150,000. He has taken $4,500 in depreciation annually leaving an exchanged basis of $105,000. If he purchased a residential replacement property with a total new basis of $165,000, his depreciation for the replacement property would be as follows: Continuation of the old schedule for remaining 17.5 years: $4,500 per year for 17.5 years. New schedule for amount of Excess Basis for 27.5 years: If depreciable improvements were deemed 80% of full value of the replacement property, then 80% of the excess basis would be depreciated over 27.5 years. The $60,000 increase in basis ($165,000 - $105,000) would be depreciated as follows: $60,000 x 80% divided by 27.5 years. The result would be $1,745 in annual depreciation to be taken for 27.5 years. The total depreciation to be taken would be $4,500 (old schedule) plus $1,745 (new schedule) for a total amount of $6,245.

10. Recovery Period.

What if the replacement property has a longer recovery period as in the exchange of residential rental property for a commercial property with a 39-year recovery period? Instead of the relinquished property depreciation allowance continuing as in our example for 17.5 years, the remaining amount of the exchanged basis to be depreciated would be spread out over the longer recovery period of 29 years (39 years minus 10 years). Unfortunately, the reverse is not true. If the exchange was from commercial to residential, the longer relinquished property depreciation schedule would continue to be used.

11. Depreciation Recapture. Explained above is how to depreciate investment or rental property that are held over the years. The taking of this depreciation (a noncash expense) reduces our ordinary income. So, when the property is sold, the IRS wants all the depreciation taken back, that is to be recaptured. However, real property in an exchange is normally Section 1250 property. If sold outright, the section 1250 property depreciation, is taxed at 25 percent. The Section 1250 depreciation taken is considered as part of the capital gain (profit +depreciation equals capital gain). So in a 1031 exchange when the capital gain is totally deferred the tax on the depreciation is also deferred. Properties that were closed before December 31, 1986 (called pre '87 properties) generally used the accelerated cost recovery method (ACRS). For these properties taxpayers claimed depreciation in excess of straight line depreciation. If sold or exchanged, the excess depreciation was taxed as ordinary income. Few properties today have excess depreciation.

12. Estimate of Depreciation. Often an owner has no idea how much depreciation was claimed on property they are thinking about exchanging. So, over the years we have developed a back of the envelope formula to estimate depreciation taken on a residential property. You take the total cost when the property was obtained, times 3%, times the number of years the property was depreciated. This gives a wild estimate to get some feel for the depreciation taken.

13. Start of Depreciation. IRS Publication 946 says depreciation is started when property is placed in service. Property is placed in service when it is ready and available for specific use. Usually this is the date of settlement. However, if a property requires repairs before it can be occupied then the date to start depreciation is the date the property is ready for use, even it a tenant has not yet leased the property.

14. Expense vs. Improvement. The owner of a property when having work done on the property has to often make the decision is it an expense that will subtracted from income or is it an improvement in which the cost will be added to my basis. It is suggested that landlords have the latest edition of Stephen Fishman's book "Every Landlord's **Tax Deduction Guide".** This book provides the latest legal guidance on what is expensed vs. an increase to basis.

Chapter 12

SECOND AND VACATION HOMES

1. **Second Home or Vacation Property.** While both are second properties, that is they are a lot or residence we own in addition to our primary residence. While all are second property, those in a vacation area are often called vacation property. They may include properties in ocean front areas, at lakes, or in the mountains. We are concerned in this Chapter primarily with the rules that qualify the second home or vacation property for a Section 1031 exchange.

Most tax practitioners and the tax court agree that when a second home is used exclusively for personal use, it does not qualify for a Section 1031 Like Kind exchange. The difference in opinion occurs when the second home or vacation home is also rented out.

There is no question that when the annual personal use of the vacation rental property is limited to 14 days or 10% of the days actually rented, whichever is greater, the property qualifies for a 1031 exchange. Annual personal use of each rental property is reported on Schedule E of IRS Form 1040. In depth instructions are contained in IRS Publication 527, 'Residential Rental Property (Including Rental of Vacation Homes)'. All involved taxpayers should have a copy of this free publication. (see Appendix for copy of Schedule E).

A main issue is if the personal use exceeds the 14 day or 10% of days actually rented rule, then the issue becomes whether the property is a non-qualifying second home or is still held for investment. IRS Section 280 establishes the rules to determine the amount of expense or loss that can be deducted annually on a vacation rental home that has excessive personal use. If personal use is exceeded then expense deductions for the year are limited to gross rental income. **If the personal use limit is not exceeded, then all the expenses may be claimed.** An exchanger should always be able to support that the property was held for investment, business or production of income. Based on use a vacation property can change from investment property status to personal use second home status from tax year to tax year. By planning ahead and restricting personal use in the year or two prior to the sale and after purchasing a qualifying replacement property, there is little question that the transaction should qualify for a 1031 exchange.

2. **Different Categories For Second Homes.** To determine which home is your principal residence, where you live the majority of the time is relatively simple as compared to the status of a second home. Over the years we have placed use of

a second home and vacation homes in various categories to try and explain their eligibility for a 1031 exchange.

These categories are:

RENTAL ONLY: It is clear that a property that is exclusively rented at a fair market value qualifies for a like-kind exchange. All operating income, expenses and depreciation are reported on Schedule E of the taxpayer's IRS Form 1040.

RENTAL WITH RESTRICTED PERSONAL USE: Personal use is within the time restrictions.as set forth in IRC Section 280A. Restricted personal use is considered as no more than 14 days or 10% of the days actually rented at a fair market rental price, whichever is greater. Such a rental would be considered as being held for business purposes under Section 1031. Thus, it is accepted within the exchange industry that a rental with restricted personal use should qualify for a like-kind exchange.

PART PERSONAL USE AND PART RENTAL USE. The controversial part of this issue occurs when the personal use exceeds the limitations., but the property is rented for part of the year. If the personal use limitations are exceeded, then the property is not considered as being held for business but could qualify as an investment property. Most practitioners maintain that section 280A does not determine if the property can qualify for a like-kind exchange. What section 280A does is establish specific rules on what tax deductions can be taken if personal use exceeds the established limits. Basically, rental expense deductions cannot exceed gross rental income. If the taxpayer has used a second home in excess of the 14 day or 10% of days actually rented, they need to recognize that the IRS may review the facts to determine if the taxpayer had a primary profit or investment motive. No one can give an assurance that the property will qualify for a like-kind exchange if the annual personal use exceeds the limitations. The taxpayer must realize in doing a 1031 exchange that the IRS may disallow the deferral of the capital gain.

PERSONAL USE – RENTAL NOT IN EXCESS OF 14 DAYS: Both a principal residence and a second home may be rented out for no greater than 14 days without the owner claiming either income or expenses. There should be no question that the primary use of the property is personal use and thus it would not qualify for a like kind exchange.

PERSONAL USE ONLY. There is no question that if a second home is used exclusively for personal use that it does not qualify for a like-kind exchange.

NO PERSONAL USE AND NO RENTAL – SECOND HOME HELD VACANT. This situation does not occur very often. If a second home is held vacant in anticipation of an increase in value, the property would be considered held for investment and should qualify for a like kind exchange. A PLR in which we were involved, qualified a 1031 relinquished property that was left vacant, clearly for investment appreciation, to be exchanged.

3. **What Is Personal Use?** The IRS definition of "personal use" is very broad. IRS Tax Topic 415 and the instructions for Schedule E of the Form 1040, describe a day of personal use of a dwelling unit as any day that it is used by:

   a. the taxpayer or any other person who has an interest in it (co-owner), unless the interest is rented to another owner as his or her main home under a shared equity financing agreement;

   b. a member of the taxpayer's family or a family member of any other person who has an interest in it, unless the family member uses it as his or her main home and pays a fair rental price.

   c. anyone under an agreement that lets the taxpayer use some other dwelling unit; or

   d. anyone, at less than fair market rental price.

Important: Any day in which the taxpayer does substantially full-time repairs or maintenance, even while others there enjoy themselves, will not be counted as a personal use day.

It is clear that in half of the categories listed above, a property may or may not qualify for use in a 1031 like-kind exchange. Unfortunately, for most vacation area second home owners, the uncertainty occurs when a property is extensively rented but personal use exceeds the 14 day or 10% of actual rental days limitation.

NOTE: To be eligible for non-recognition treatment, that is deferral of capital gain, under section 1031 the second home must be held by the taxpayer for either productive use in trade or business, or for investment, and not as a personal residence.

4. **Safe Harbor IRS Revenue Procedure 2008-16.** For a long time the QI and accounting industries had been asking the IRS for guidance on the circumstances necessary for a vacation home to qualify for a 1031 exchange without any questions being asked or fear of an audit. Thus, IRS Revenue Procedure 2008-16 was drafted

effective for exchanges of dwelling units occurring on or after March 10, 2008. The purpose of the Revenue Procedure 2008-16 is to provide a Safe Harbor under which the IRS will not challenge whether a dwelling unit with limited personal use qualifies as property held for productive use in a trade or business or for investment for purposes of Section 1031 of the IRC.

The Revenue Procedure says, "The Service recognizes that many taxpayers hold dwelling units primarily for the production of current rental income, but also use the properties occasionally for personal purposes." The Revenue Procedure applies to a dwelling unit that meets the Qualifying Use Standards.

For this Revenue Procedure, a dwelling unit is real property improved with a house, apartment, condominium, or similar accommodations including sleeping space, bathroom and cooking facilities.

The Qualifying Use Standards established in Section 4 of this Revenue Procedure are unique. If the standards are met, the IRS will not challenge whether the dwelling unit is held for a qualifying use in an exchange. The Qualifying Use Standards apply to both the relinquished property and the replacement property.

The Qualifying Use Standards set forth in Revenue Procedure 2008-16 are:

a. that the dwelling unit with limited personal use is owned at least 24 months before the exchange if it's the relinquished property, or 24 months after the exchange if it's the replacement property.

b. that, within the applicable 24 month qualifying use period, in each of the two 12-month periods, the taxpayer rents the dwelling unit to another unrelated person or persons at fair value rental for 14 days or more. A related person may rent at fair market value if the dwelling unit is a principal residence for the related person and there is a share equity agreement.

c. that the property must be a dwelling unit. A taxpayer utilizing the Safe Harbor in this Revenue Procedure also must satisfy all other requirements for a like-kind exchange under Section 1031 and the regulations there under. In accordance with Section 4.03 of the Rev. Proc. and IRC Section 280A(d)(2), if any related person or a person who has an interest in such a unit is allowed to use the vacation house, even if they rent it at a fair market rent, it is considered personal use.

d. While the Rev. Proc. provides a Safe Harbor for those who meet all its provisions. An exchange may still fall outside these specific parameters and yet still meet the statutory requirements for an exchange. If you want to use the Safe Harbor, the revenue procedure looks at each property to determine if personal use is too high and if actual rental income is generated. If you have a relinquished dwelling with personal use, we now know to avoid IRS challenge of the exchange that you should own it 2 years before an exchange, rent it to someone other than direct family at fair value for at least 14 days in each of the 2 years, and limit personal use to 14 days or 10% of the days rented, whichever is larger.

The same logic applies if the dwelling unit is your replacement property, you must own the replacement 2 years after an exchange, rent it to someone other than direct family person at fair value at least 14 days in each of the 2 years, and limit personal use to 14 days or 10% of the days rented, whichever is larger.

The Revenue Procedure 2008-16, is contained in the Appendix in this book and should be reviewed if you think your exchange will be within the Safe Harbor rules.

Note: Danger — there are no current instructions as to when the taxpayer has to claim that the exchange meets the safe harbor rules. This should only be necessary if the IRS challenges that the reported 1031 exchange does not qualify. If a taxpayer reports an exchange based on the expectation that a dwelling unit will meet the qualifying use standards of the Revenue Procedure, it unfortunately states in Section 4.05 of the Procedure that if the exchanger "subsequently determines that the dwelling unit does not meet the qualifying use standards, the taxpayer, if necessary, should file an amended return and **not** report the transaction as an exchange under Section 1031."

5. **Rental Outside the Safe Harbor.** While it is unfortunate that most rental vacation properties do not meet the Safe Harbor provisions, it is possible that such properties can qualify for a 1031 exchange. It is important to recognize that the conditions given in the Rev. Proc. are very conservative and regardless a rental residence that meets such conditions would certainly qualify for a 1031 exchange. Vacation homes outside the Safe Harbor Rev. Proc. criteria, used by the taxpayer for personal use and are frequently rented can also be exchanged. These vacation homes need to be considered held for investment or in a trade or business. Unfortnately there is no test or criteria outside the Safe Harbor Rev. Proc. that determines when a vacation property is held primarily for investment purposes and therefore qualifies for a 1031 exchange.

An owner should always have the necessary records/documents on file to prove to the IRS in case of an audit that profit was the motive in owning the vacation property. Expenses, depreciation, and interest paid should be always properly claimed.

6. **Conversion to Principal Residence.** The conversion of your vacation or rental property into your principal residence is very simple. You simply move in and declare it as your principal residence. You can only have one principal residence at the same time. The time limits and rules for sale and exclusion of gain for a principal residence are contained in IRC Section 121, as amended, and the IRS regulations on section 121. These rules are covered in Chapter 18 of this book.

Chapter 13

1031 STRATEGIES

1. **Introduction.** In other chapters we have explained the many types of exchanges which are most common. In this chapter we cover some other types of situations and 1031 strategies taxpayers are implementing. While most often an exchanger who desires a replacement property on which will be built or remodeled the investment or business property will do a reverse exchange as covered in Chapter 10. With the EAT or selected party supervising the new construction.

2. **Improvement on Owned Property.** In addition to the reverse exchange a situation can occur when a taxpayer/exchanger desires that a rental house or other improvement be built on their replacement property. The most common situation is when the taxpayer has a contract on the property they are selling (the property to be relinquished) and wish to purchase a replacement property unimproved lot and have a house built on it. Often a taxpayer will plan to take title to the replacement property lot, and then contract to have a house built on the lot.

<u>If the taxpayer takes title to the lot, the exchange is complete (done), and any additional improvements are not like-kind.</u>

In most cases, the purchase price for the lot will not satisfy the reinvestment requirements for the exchange. If the price of the lot is equal to or greater than the adjusted sale price of the relinquished property, then only the lot needs to be purchased and the exchange is completed.

Otherwise, a builder or a **non-related** third party must purchase the lot, take title and start construction. If the taxpayer already has a contract on a replacement property lot, it must be assigned to the third party or the builder. The taxpayer may lend the funds or guarantee the loan of the third party or builder to purchase the property and start construction. The third party or builder must not be an agent of the taxpayer. The third party or builder should have economic risk at stake in the purchase of the land and building of the improvements. Then the taxpayer has a real estate purchase contract prepared which provides for the taxpayer to purchase from the third party or builder the replacement property lot with a house built thereon to their specifications. The contract should provide for transfer of the property before the end of the 180 day exchange period. The contract may also provide for the payment of additional deposits by the QI or the taxpayer as construction progress is made. After the relinquished property goes to settlement, the Qualified Intermediary will be holding exchange escrow funds which may be used toward the purchase of the replacement property. Once the real estate purchase contract for the replacement property is assigned to the Qualified Intermediary. The exchange escrow funds may be disbursed by the Qualified Intermediary in accordance with the contract.

In a to-be-built exchange within 45 days of the transfer of the relinquished property the taxpayer/exchanger must provide the proper identification. The regulation is unclear as to the detail required, but a prudent taxpayer would provide as much detail as they can.

The exchanger must receive the replacement property within the 180 day exchange period. The replacement property received must be "substantially" the same property as identified. If the construction is not complete by the 180th day, the property must be transferred to the QI and the exchanger. The property received will be considered to be substantially the same property as identified only if, had production been completed, it would have been considered as substantially the same property as identified. The exchange value transferred should be adjusted by the value of the work not completed.

An option is to lease the land to the contractor or third party for a term in excess of 30 years plus the time required to complete the construction of the desired improvements. A lease of real estate for over thirty years, including options, is considered real property and thus qualifies as a replacement property.

The contractor or third party constructs the improvements on the leasehold, and then conveys the lessee's interest in the ground lease and the ownership of the improvements to the taxpayer as replacement property. There must be at least 30 years remaining on the lease when it is conveyed back to the taxpayer.

3. Shared Equity Financing Agreement. Recently, a nationally syndicated real estate columnist was asked "if we sell our rental property can we avoid capital gains if we help our daughter purchase a place to live".

The answer was – tough break you will have to pay the capital gains tax when you sell your rental. This of course is not a complete answer. Mom and Pop can do a 1031 like-kind exchange and purchase with their daughter an interest in her new home. This type exchange and purchase requires a **'shared equity financing agreement'** in addition to the 1031 exchange documentation. This agreement is required by the IRS because the personal use of a home by a co-owner may disqualify the property as an investment property unless there is a 'shared equity financing agreement'. If the exchanger plans to purchase with a co-owner a replacement property in which the co-owner will live, it is essential that they have such a written agreement. Without this Agreement, the IRS will treat the property as a personal use second home. As such, it may not qualify as a rental or an exchange replacement property. Most real estate professionals are not familiar with this requirement and few attorneys have experience preparing such an agreement. Thus, if you are planning to co-own your investment property with an occupant, we strongly recommend you obtain help from a knowledgeable attorney.

4. Installment Sale and Treatment of Note from Buyer.

Often an exchanger must take back a Promissory Note from the buyer in order to dispose of the relinquished property. Two different approaches may be taken. These approaches are: One, at settlement the exchanger receives the Note directly from the buyer. The value of the Note becomes boot as non-like property and may be treated as an installment sale. Second, at settlement the Qualified Intermediary receives the Note directly from the buyer. That is, the Note is made payable to the Qualified Intermediary. The Note then becomes part of the qualified escrow held by the Qualified Intermediary and can be disposed of as follows:

a. The exchanger can arrange and the QI can sell the Note, to a third party, and add the proceeds to the other cash in the qualified escrow account (no boot to exchanger), or

b. The Note can be used as part of the compensation for the purchase of the replacement property (no boot to exchanger). At settlement the Note is endorsed to the seller of the replacement property to the QI, or

c. If the Note matures in less than 180 days, the Qualified Intermediary places the payoff in the qualified escrow account, (no boot to exchanger) and uses the funds toward purchase of the replacement property, or:

d. At the time of settlement of the replacement property, the exchanger can purchase the Note from the Qualified Intermediary (no boot to exchanger). The cash received is used by the QI toward the purchase of the replacement property; or

e. After the exchange, the Note is endorsed by the Qualified Intermediary to the exchanger and the Note can be reported as an installment sale. A Note may be either payable to the exchanger or QI and still qualify as an installment sale.

Note: While holding the Note the Qualified Intermediary must collect interest and comply with all other provisions set forth in the Note.

5. Combining IRC Sections 121 and 1031. Often a sale will include both a business property and a principal residence. A farm is good example of such a situation. You can think of many such examples, including a business where the family lives above the store, or a principle residence where there is an area devoted to a home business endeavor. The combining Section 121, covering a principal residence, and Section 1031, covering a business, investment property, or rental is covered in IRS Revenue Procedure 2005-14.

6. Auctions. Very little has been written about doing a 1031 exchange which involves an auction of the relinquished or replacement property. However, a 1031 exchange may take place if auction properties are involved. Remember, the same 1031 documentation required for a regular 1031 exchange is required if an auctioned property is involved.

If you plan to conduct an auction of the investment or business property you own, then doing a 1031 exchange by reinvesting in a qualifying replacement property it is not necessary to have the Exchange and Escrow Account Agreement in place before the auction. Nor is it necessary to have the fact you plan to do a 1031 exchange in the auction advertisement, or even initially tell the winning bidder you plan to do a 1031 exchange. The difference you will notice is a signed copy of the advertisement by the winning bidder may serve as the contract for the sale and purchase of the property. Once you have a winning bidder than the Exchange and Escrow Account Agreement must be prepared quickly to the QI, along with the required assignment documentation. The auction company and the Attorney listed in the advertisement and the settlement agent must be notified of the Exchange and Escrow Account Agreement and assignment.

When the auctioned property goes to settlement, or is transferred, the 45-day ID and 180 exchange periods start as normal. After settlement, the exchange escrow funds will be wired separately by the QI. **The exchanger should not collect the funds.**

Frequently, the exchanger has sold his property normally and is in the 45-day ID period, or prior to settlement, when he finds a property being auctioned, and he wins the bid for the property. The same basic process is followed. The signed advertisement may serve as the contract for the auctioned property. An assignment and settlement instructions will be prepared by the QI, and all parties involved will be notified. When the date for settlement, or transfer, of the replacement property arrives (this may be a very short period) the QI will arrange to have the bank wire the required escrow funds. The situation may also arise where the taxpayer finds an auction property he desires but has not sold or even listed his current property. In that case after a winning bid he may desire to use a Reverse Exchange, to get control of the new property. The EAT will purchase the desired property, then the taxpayer can put the relinquished property on the market and within 180 days sell the property, and complete the 1031 exchange by buying and transferring the property held by the EAT.

It is wise, when an exchanger after the settlement of the relinquished property, is going to ID an auction property, that additional properties also be ID in accordance with the 45-day ID rules. This is done to protect the taxpayer options in case he does not win the bidding on the auctioned property. Normally the auction company is not concerned if the property is an exchange, as the goal of getting a good buyer at the bid price has been accomplished, regardless if the EAT is on title or a QI is involved. If you are planning to sell or buy an auction property it is wise to discuss your plans as early as possible with the QI you are using.

7. Dealer Property. While many taxpayers would like to do a 1031 exchange, if is determined that they have property that is considered 'dealer property' - they cannot do a 1031 exchange. If an entity is holding property "primarily for sale in the ordinary course of business" it makes the property - dealer property. Many factors are considered when declaring property as 'dealer property'.

Each property is considered on its own. Thus, an entity may have individual lots for sale that are considered dealer property, while at the same time they are holding a rental house that qualifies for a 1031 exchange.

If a property is considered dealer property the tax treatment can be significantly different, therefore taxpayers should get tax advice if it is considered a property should qualify for capital gain or for a 1031 exchange.

8. Suspended Passive Losses. IRC Section 469(c)(2) establishes all rental property as a passive activity. This section applies to all individuals, estates, trusts, closely held corporations, and personal service corporations. There are two kinds of passive activity. These are a trade or business in which you do not materially participate, and rental activities, regardless of your participation, unless you are a real estate professional.

IRS Publication 527 covers in detail the limits on rental losses if you had excessive personal use of the property.

Real Estate Professional. If you qualify as a real estate professional, rental real estate activities in which you materially participate are **not** passive activities. You qualify as a real estate professional for the year if you meet both of the following requirements: first, one half of all business services performed were in real property businesses in which you materially participated, and second, you performed more than 750 hours in real property businesses. For a full explanation of this very favorable rule, see IRS Publication 925.

Special Allowance. If you and/or your spouse actively participated in a passive rental real estate activity, you can deduct up to $25,000 of **loss** from the activity from your non-passive income. This special allowance is an exception to the general rule disallowing **losses** in excess of income from passive activities. The maximum $25,000 allowance is reduced if your modified adjusted gross income (MAGI) exceeds $100,000 and you are married filing jointly.

If you do not qualify for the special allowance and rental property expenses and depreciation exceed the rental income these losses become suspended passive losses and are reported on IRS Form 8582, Passive Activity Loss Limitations, (see Instructions for Form 8582). Then all of the suspended losses for that activity can be used to offset the recognized gain from the sale of the property. A fully taxable transaction is one in which you recognize all the realized gain. Gains from other passive activities can offset losses from rental real estate.

If the rental property being exchanged has significant realized gain, then the best option may be to do a 1031 exchange and use the suspended loss on that property. How does this work? Let's say you have accumulated $20,000 in suspended losses on the property in the current and /or past years. At settlement you can receive $20,000 from the settlement agent thus creating $20,000 in cash boot.

Or you can reinvest $20,000 less than the cash received from the relinquished property. At the end of the exchange the qualified intermediary will arrange to have you sent the $20,000. This is recognized cash boot. Any boot recognized in the exchange transfer of the property is considered passive activity gain that can be used to offset suspended passive losses. This is reported by completing Schedule E to determine the loss or gain for the current year.

If the property is not sold outright or boot recognized, then your third option is to do nothing and any suspended passive losses not used will be carried forward to the replacement property.

9. **Delaware Statuary Trust (DST).** For many investors who wish to reduce daily management responsibilities the DST is a strategy to consider. It has taken the place for many investors of the TIC commercial investments previously considered. In Revenue Ruling 2004-86 the IRS recognized that a taxpayer may exchange qualifying real property for an interest in a Delaware Statuary Trust (DST) in a 1031 exchange. The DST is set up under Delaware law and is used by investors who wish reduced management responsibilities. The revenue ruling provides specific IRS guidance and conditions for a DST. A DST provides that while the owner does not receive a deed, he does have a percentage ownership in a trust that owns real property. There is no limit on the number of investors in a DST. The only right of an investor is to receive DST distributions. The investor may not have any voting rights. Since lenders only look to the DST as the single borrower, it is easier and less expensive for the DST to get financing. It is possible to do a 1031 exchange out of a DST.

While the use of a QI is still required an exchanger should fully understand what they will receive, what their rights are, and the fees in a DST.

10. Triple New Lease.

Another strategy to reduce daily management concerns is the 'Triple Net Lease' (NNN) property. This type of commercial lease requires the tenant to pay some or all the expenses. These expenses can include taxes, maintenance, repairs, insurance, and utilities as set forth in the lease. Such leases are normally for longer terms, are renewable by the tenant, and may provide for a rent escalator clause. An investor can both do a 1031 exchange into or out of a net lease property. The lease terms just have to be always honored by the new owner.

11. Conservation or Scenic Easement.

A taxpayer can sell the rights, normally by perpetual easement, to their property to someone, normally a non-profit or government agency, who wants to preserve it or the scenic view for prosperity. An easement is a right in real property and the granting of a perpetual easement may be like kind to a fee interest in real estate. So a property owner following 1031 exchange rules can have any cash or credits received for the easement sent to the QI and purchase as a replacement property a like-kind fee interest in real estate.

12. Refinance of Replacement Property. Sometimes a potential exchanger is upset when he is advised that all the cash received from the relinquished property(ies) should be reinvested in the replacement property(ies). Many times they owe nothing on the relinquished property and wish to pull out some cash tax free and get a mortgage to purchase the replacement property.

While the exchanger should reinvest all the cash received, they can after settlement refinance the property tax free in order to obtain cash. Emphasis is placed on the need for time to pass after settlement of the replacement property. If the refinance occurs too close to settlement, or prior to settlement loan arrangement are made, the IRS may disallow the 1031 exchange.

13. Gas, Oil and Mineral Right Exchanges. A 1031 exchange can be used when selling or buying certain oil, gas and mineral rights. The IRS has held that a royalty interest in oil and gas in place is an interest in real property for tax purposes. Such a replacement property purchase may provide an exchanger with diversification and monthly royalty payments. Such 1031 exchanges are a specialty and exchangers want to be certain the QI has knowledge and experience with this type of exchange.

14. Property Subdivision and 1031 Exchange.

If you subdivided a piece of land and even if you made some improvements such as roads, water and drainage facilities, you can still do a 1031 exchange. Details are contained in IRC Section 1237, and IRS regulation §1.1237-1 thereto. It is important not to be considered a dealer or have recently undertaken sales activity. The property needs to be considered investment property and not 'for sale lots'.

15. Timber Exchange.

Another type of 1031 exchange which gets attention in some parts of country is that involving timber. There are two situations which can effect timber land. The first is the sale and deferred exchange of capital gain of land, with standing timber. This land must have been held in a trade or business or as an investment. Such land is considered real property and can be exchanged for other real estate.

The second involves a timber deed which gives a person the right to cut and remove the timber for a specific number of years. State law determines if such is real or personal property. Timberland not held in a trade or business or for investment may not qualify for a 1031exchange. It is not clear, regardless of the state law or period of cutting allowed, that a timber deed qualifies the seller to exchange it for another property in a 1031 exchange. In all transactions involving timber the owner should consult with a local CPA or tax attorney to see exactly what is the state law and for what type tax treatment the land and timber may qualify.

16. Estate Taxes. If a person dies the federal estate tax law, which applies to all deceased persons, is imposed. The provisions of the estate tax laws are totally separate from any other laws, such as IRC §1031. As the estate tax laws are changed frequently, those concerned should check for the current rules.

The value of all the property owned by the decedent, be it real property, stocks, or other assets, is subject to the estate tax laws. Property that was received by the decedent in a 1031 exchange is not treated differently than all other property.

For estates larger than the federally exempted amount, any estate tax due must be paid. The value of any 1031 exchange property is included in the estate.

All persons who inherit any type of property, including real estate or stocks, receive it at Fair Market Value (FMV), that then becomes the staring basis for the property when it is sold. When a person inherits any property at FMV, all gain escapes capital gain taxation. By law then, even a so-called 1031 property is inherited at FMV. While the value of all property is included in the estate subject to taxation, no unrealized gain, including §1031 deferred gains, is taxable to the heirs.

As noted, when a person inherits property their new basis is the FMV, but if they receive it as a gift their basis is that of the donor.

When desired, a heir using the FMV as a starting basis, can do a 1031 exchange.

Thus: it is better to inherit property, then receive it as a gift.

17. Conclusion. This chapter has tried to mention those 1031 exchange strategies that can be used in addition to the more popular type exchanges which have their own chapter. Also covered have some items that may also be of interest to 1031 exchangers. Additional items of interest relative to a 1031 exchange are covered in Exchange Miscellany in Chapter 17.

Chapter 14

DECLARED DISASTERS AND OFFICIAL DUTY IN COMBAT AREAS

1. **Declared Disasters.** We continue to have many disasters of all types in the United States. The people are dealing with hurricanes, floods, fires, and other disasters. We learn on the evening news of the disaster, and likely that the governor has declared a disaster.

However, for the relinquished property 45 identification date or for the180 day completion date to be extended – the disaster has to be a Presidential Declared Disaster area.

2. **IRS Press Releases.** We will hear of many disaster areas but only a few are declared Presidential Declared Disaster areas. The declaration may also come many days after the actual disaster date. The easiest way to check if a property is included, is to go to IRS site 'Tax Relief in Disaster Situation'. It will show the disaster number, and most important the **counties** in the declared disaster area. As additional counties may be added later, concerned parties should continue to recheck the news release.

Note: Not all federally declared disaster areas will receive the tax extension deadline relief.

3. **Extension of ID and Exchange Period End Dates.** Only if stated in the declaration can the reliefs provided in Revenue Procedure 2018-58 be used. Section 17 of the revenue procedure provides the postponements parameters. The 45-day ID period, the 180 day exchange period that occur after the presidentially declared disaster are normally postponed 120 days. But not later then the due date of the taxpayer's return or one year.

4. **QI Coordination.** If an extension is taken by the exchanger it should be coordinated with the QI so that the suspense dates are amended in writing.

5. **Affected Taxpayers.** The Rev. Proc. lists the conditions for taxpayers who may be 'affected' and provides that others may qualify for the extension if they can show they had difficulty meeting the exchange deadlines due to the disaster.

6. Combat Zone Service. Revenue Procedure 2018-58 also provides that exchange and QEEA time periods are postponed for military service in a combat zone. The period of military combat service and 180 days thereafter are disregarded in computing time period under §1031.

Chapter 15

FEDERAL AND STATE ACTIVITY

1. **Federal Activity.** As previously noted, the major Federal activity was the was the amendment of basic 1031 law in the TCJA. This amendment eliminated private property exchanges but kept real property (real estate) exchanges. Another important federal action was the release of IRS Revenue Procedure 2019-38. It provides 'safe harbor' provisions under which a real estate enterprise will be treated as a trade or business for section 199A deductions. IRC section 199A provides up to a 20% deduction of qualified business income for non-corporation taxpayers. Real estate rentals personally used the **greater** of 14 days or 10% of the days rented cannot use the 'safe harbor'. A deduction may still be claimed outside the 'safe harbor' but may be subject to IRS scrutiny.

   It is anticipated that IRS will publish new section 1031 regulations to reflect the changes made by the TCJA. They will most likely provide a definition of 'real property'.

2. **State Activity.** The FEA has been very active in many states to promote the adoption of the FEA drafted model. At least 10 states have adopted or considered the model law that has shaped their approach to regulation of exchanges and influenced state taxation and procedures for exchange transactions. These laws primarily help protect consumers. Exchangers should be aware if their state has such a law and what procedures protect them. The FEA model law covers many topics, including QI insurance, bonding, security of escrow funds, advertising truthfulness and QI ownership.

3. **State Conformity.** Not all states have changed their state tax laws to be in conformity with the Federal 1031 law (i.e. no personal property exchanges). Concerned exchangers should check in advance relative to state conformity.

4. **Virginia QI Law.** Based on the FEA model law and referred to as the 'VA QI Law'. The original law was effective July 1, 2010. The full title of the law was an amendment to Title 55 of the Code of Virginia which added 'Chapter 27.1, Exchange Facilitators Act'. The law, without change, was renumbered in October 2019 and is now 'Title 55.1, Chapter 8, sections 55.1-800 through 55.1-806'.

The law applies to all property being exchange and located in Virginia, a QI with an office in VA, a QI facilitating a VA 1031 exchange, and an EAT taking title to VA property.

5. Maryland Withholding. Exchangers who are out-of-State residents, and do not have an exception, have had some of their relinquished property proceeds withheld at settlement. The current withholding rate if 8% of the estimated profit. Other States are also withholding some proceeds at settlement. So, exchangers should check in advance. This is particularly important if required State taxes have not been filed.

6. California Claw-Back. The Franchise Tax Board (FTB) in California has been very aggressive in their review of 1031 exchanges. Now, exchangers who transfer California property for non-Calif. property in a 1031 exchange must file an annual form with the FTB. If the non-California property is eventually sold (not transferred in a 1031 exchange), it is expected that the original tax on deferred gain earned in California will be paid (the claw-back provision).

Example: Kevin does a 1031 exchange of a CA rental and defers $100,000 of capital gain earned in CA. His replacement property is in a non-CA State. He sells the property years later and has $200,000 of capital gain. California expects (claw-back) the original deferred tax on the $100,000 of the gain to be paid back to them.

Exchangers should be aware that other revenue hungry States may follow the CA example.

Chapter 16

REPORTING THE EXCHANGE

1. **Reporting Form.** The exchange is reported on IRS Form 8824 and attached to your normal tax return. Regardless of the year the replacement property is received, the exchange is always reported for the year the first relinquished property was transferred.

2. **Receipt of Replacement Property in Following Year.** If the replacement property is received in the following (second) year, the final tax return should not be filed until all replacement property is received or the exchange period has ended.

3. **On-time Extension.** If you will receive the replacement property after the **due date** for your return, you must file an on-time extension (Form 4868) to get the full 180 days.

4. **Completing Form 8824.** The form 8824 is very complicated and uses terms which most exchangers are not familiar. Therefore, CPAs or other tax prepares may be used to complete the form. If a taxpayer desires the advanced versions of Turbo Tax can compute and print out the form, showing you the gain, the capital gain deferred, and the starting basis for the replacement property.

5. **No ID Submitted.** If a taxpayer starts an exchange, but does not identify replacement property by the 45th day, he receives the escrow funds from the QI, does not complete a form 8824, but reports the transfer of the relinquished property as a sale, and pays all the taxes.

6. **Cash in Following Year.** If you do not complete the exchange and receive cash from the QI in the following year you may file IRS form 6252, 'Installment Sale', with your return. The tax on the cash received will then be due with your tax return for the year the cash was received.

7. **Instructions.** Instructions on how to complete Form 8824 and a final current form are published by the IRS late in each year. A draft form 8824 may be available from the IRS in mid-year.

Chapter 17

EXCHANGE MISCELLANY

1. **Introduction.** Since 1990 when the Section 1031(k)-1 Regulation was published, which made the like kind exchange process simpler, and more popular, there has been a lot of activity by the IRS, States, and the Congress to add rules and attempt to further clarify the process. A review of the many topics covered in the paragraphs of this book will point out the multitude of actions over time that impacted in some way on 1031 exchanges. Some of these actions impact on only a few people, and like the Private Letter Rulings (PLR) are only applicable to them, and can only be cited by the party requesting the PLR. But they provide a good indicator of Treasury and IRS thinking on a particular subject. It will be apparent reading this chapter it was very difficult to include some topics in a given chapter, and thus they have been placed in this miscellaneous chapter. Perhaps we should call it the "catch all" chapter.

2. **Failed QI.** In March 2010, the IRS published Rev. Proc. 2010-14 to provide a safe harbor method, of reporting gain or loss, for certain taxpayers who initiated deferred like-kind exchanges under §1031 of the IRC but fail to complete the exchange because a qualified intermediary (QI) defaulted. The industry had been concerned that sellers who were trying to do an exchange, and then had a QI who took their exchange funds or placed them where they were not liquid, and then went bankrupt, would have to pay capital gains on the property they sold as a relinquished property but did not receive all of their escrow funds back. This Rev. Proc. basically solves that problem.

3. **Bank QI Merger Issue.** In PLR 201030020, issued in July 2010, the IRS stated "the QI which is the transferee of the relinquished property and the QI which is the transferor of the replacement property must be the same person". In other words, you can't change QIs in the middle of an exchange. With the merger of so many banks, it is not surprising that a bank was going to ask if they were going to be considered the same QI after the merger with another bank who was acting as a QI. Even if they were the bank holding the escrow funds, the QI would be considered to be the same person after the merger. Since this ruling was related to bank rules, it is not possible to know if other types of QI mergers would be treated in the same fashion.

4. **Contract for Deed.** The contract for deed, also known as an installment land contract, is different in that it combines treatment as a change of ownership and an installment sale. So often we are asked since it a change of ownership, can I do a 1031 exchange? The answer is a simple no. In a contract for deed the contract buyer gets to occupy the property, while paying as required in the contract, toward the property purchase price. When all the payments required are made, then the seller transfers the deed to the buyer.

The IRS considers a contract for deed as a sale, and the buyer has all the tax advantages of ownership, including deductibility as mortgage and interest payments are made. The seller reports the payments received as an installment sale on Form 6252, paying on the share of capital gains as necessary. The seller cannot claim depreciation or other ownership benefits.

Since the seller retains legal title to the property, and receives installment payments, he cannot do a 1031 exchange. Nor can he do a 1031 exchange when the final payment is made.

5. **Self-Directed IRA.** There are a number of financial companies who are promoting self-directed IRA investments in real estate. The primary reason the property does not qualify for a 1031 exchange is that the entity buying or selling the property is not the tax payer but the custodian/trustee holding the IRA assets. In a 1031 exchange the taxpayer must hold both the relinquished property and the replacement property. In a self-directed IRA any profit on the sale or operation of the property is placed in the IRA by the custodian and is invested as directed by the investor.

6. **Development Rights.** In January 2009, the IRS released PLR-121709-08, which stated that development rights could be like-kind to a fee interest in real estate. In this case the taxpayer did a 1031 exchange of development rights (ex: pertaining to residential density) for other development rights (pertaining to hotel development).

7. **Cost Segregation.** This is a valuation study conducted on commercial or multifamily real estate to identify and value the different parts of a property for depreciation purposes. Certain components of a property, like the elevators may have a shorter life recovery period and higher depreciation write off then the real estate itself. These higher depreciation schedules will increase the depreciation expenses and bottom line of the property involved. For current property this can be an attractive tax saving step. Cost segregation has been an approved action since the late nineties.

However, the study makes parts of the real estate into section 1245 property, with a faster depreciated rate. It has been estimated that 10 to 15% of an office building can be reclassified in a cost segregation study.

8. **Section 468b and 7872.** For some years the exchange industry was waiting for the IRS and the Treasury to modify regulations Sections 468B and 7872 to cover exchange escrow funds and below market loans. The final published amendments have minimal impact on exchangers and follow the positions advocated by the FEA.

The final amended regulations published in T.D. 9413 in 2008 exempt exchanges from Section 7872 if the escrow funds treated as loaned are $2 million or less and the funds are held for 6 months or less. More important, Par. 3. Section 1.468B-6(c)(2) was added to the regulation and provided that exchange escrow funds are not treated as loan to the QI if in accordance with the exchange and escrow agreement: all the earnings (ex: interest) attributable to exchange escrow funds are paid to the taxpayer, and if the exchange funds are held in a separately identified account, in a depository institution, under the taxpayer's name and tax identity number.

As before the exchanger must treat interest funds earned on the escrow account as interest income and pay taxes as required.

9. **Exchange of Leasehold.** This PLR (200842019), along with some other items, ruled that exchange of leaseholds are like-kind even if the leases might vary in their terms or value.

10. **Partnership Exchanges.** First find out how your present investment property is titled/deeded. You may get a surprise. Is it deeded to you personally, to each couple, to a partnership, or to an LLC? As a team, you may have considered yourselves partners, but how the property is titled/deeded down at the county courthouse is what is important in a 1031 exchange. Let's say you find it is titled in each of your individual names. You are in luck. You own an interest in property which you can sell and if the property qualifies do a 1031 exchange using the name on the title. This is important because a 1031 exchange must be done, with minor exceptions, using the same name as on the title/deed of the property interest to be relinquished.

If it is titled as a "partnership" there are some actions required. First look at IRC §761(A) which lets partners involved in an investment property to not be taxed as a partnership, but as individuals, then look at a partnership "drop and swap". In the Section 1031 law it clearly states "an interest in a partnership which has in effect a valid election under section 761(a) to be excluded from the application of all of subchapter K shall be treated as an interest in each of the assets of such partnership and not as an interest in a partnership."

If the property is titled to a partnership and it files a partnership return the first course of action is to file a IRC Section 761(A) waiver. The 761(A) waiver seems designed for investors who are only owners of a single residential investment property. The 761(A) election permits a partnership tax-wise to avoid being treated as a partnership. Co-owners file their share of the income and expenses on Schedule E of their individual returns. Exclusion from the subchapter K treatment then allows all members to do a 1031 exchange of their interest. If necessary, the actions for the 761(A) waiver or for the following "drop and swap" should be started as far in advance as possible.

While there are other methods to dissolve a partnership the "drop and swap" seems the most common. In this procedure the partnership is terminated and the assets are distributed to the partners. The partners should then own and operate the property as tenants in common" for as long a period of time as possible. Each former partner will be filing their taxes separately. While there are no IRS guidelines how long the property is held individually, one year is normally suggested, with the "longer the better" understood. This is the "drop" portion and then after a while you can "swap" – do a 1031 exchange of your interest by selling to your co-owners or a third party and getting a replacement property. If your co-owners just buy you out and you do not do a 1031 exchange you will have to pay a tax on all your gain above basis, including the recapture of all the depreciation allowed.

Hopefully, your share of the property will qualify for a 1031 exchange and you will be able to defer the capital gains tax. Having the property titled/deeded in individual names will also be to the advantage of your co-owners who may someday also want to sell their interest and do a 1031 exchange.

Have no doubt that dissolution of a partnership is risky and good legal advice should be sought as early as possible.

11. Sale and Leaseback. Is a commercial real estate transaction where the owner sells the property and signs a long-term lease (usually a NNN lease) with the buyer. Investor exchangers are also buying replacement properties from the owners, getting a long-term lease, and not having to search for a new tenant. Often times the owner is a large national company, who rather lease their stores, etc. and use the cash to obtain new locations.

12. Flipping Properties. Many investors are involved with buying a foreclosure or other cheap residential house, fixing it up, and immediately trying to sell it. They want to do a 1031 exchange. But normally they do not qualify for a 1031 exchange because they are not holding the property for investment, but for sale.

13. IRC Section 1033 – Involuntary Conversions. If a property owner has to dispose of a property due to destruction, theft, or under threat of condemnation or taking by eminent domain no gain is recognized if similar property or one "related in service or use" is obtained.

While the §1033 deferral provisions are more liberal than the rules for a 1031 exchange, some taxpayers may desire to follow §1031 rules and obtain a like-kind property instead of a similar property. *Example: an office building instead of a residential rental house.*

The Section 1033 rules provide a longer replacement period, do not require mortgage liability, and do not require a QI. If an involuntary conversion is possible or pending the owner should consult a tax advisor to learn of the rules that will be involved.

14. Like-Kind Exchange and Installment Sale. Frequently a taxpayer doing a 1031 exchange of the relinquished property will be asked by the buyer to take back a certain amount of the price as an installment sale. A 1031 exchange may be combined with an Installment sale. It does not manner if the Note is made payable to the seller or the QI.

Example: An exchanger offers the relinquished property for $500,000. The buyer accepts the price, but request the owner take-back $100,000 as an installment sale.

The exchanger needs to purchase replacement property for at least the net sales price of $400,000 to defer the remaining Capital Gain on the relinquished property. The exchanger will then pay tax on the gain as received from the installment sale. Any interest received in also taxed. See installment sale instructions in IRS Publication 537.

Chapter 18

1031 AND CONVERSION TO PRINCIPAL RESIDENCE

1. **Introduction.** Frequently a property held as a rental is converted to a taxpayers' principal residence (often called a main home). The reverse is also true when the home owner converts their home to rental, for example because of a job change, rather than sell the home. This chapter will cover the more complex situation where a property is received in a 1031 exchange and converted to a principal residence and then later sold under the principal residence exclusion rules of IRC §121.

2. **Conversion.** When a principal residence is converted to a rental or vice-versus there is no tax – **it is a tax free change**. The principal residence is still owned but is now a rental property. IRS Form 1040, Schedule E, is used to report income, expenses and depreciation when the property is ready and available.

3. **1031 Exchange Received Property.** A common 1031 exchange strategy is to exchange investment property for another qualifying property in a location that the exchanger may eventually want to live. For example, an exchanger may exchange a rental townhouse in an urban area like Washington, D.C. for a beach property in the Outer Banks of NC with no intent that it will become his personal residence. The basic exchange rules require that both properties, relinquished and replacement, be held for business or investment purposes. After renting the replacement property long enough to clearly show that the replacement property qualified as investment property or production of income, a taxpayer can then do what they want with the property. A taxpayer may hope to eventually move into the investment property, converting it to their principal residence. Taxpayers may plan that this will be their final home. But there will always be situations where the home has to be sold after it has been converted to a primary residence.

4. **Selling a Home Taxation Rules.** When you sell your principal residence, regardless of its location, the gain/profit on the sale, up to $250,000 for singles, or $500,000 for joint filers, will be **excluded** from your income if you meet the **use** and **ownership** tests. These rules are established in IRC Section 121 "Exclusion of Gain from Sale of Principal Residence", related regulations and Pub 523.

To qualify for the principal residence exclusion a taxpayer will have had to live in the property for at least two years (a total of 730 days) during the past five years period. Short temporary absences, such as vacations, are counted as periods of use.

You as the taxpayer, or your spouse, have used the home as a primary residence for two years, anytime during the past five years, and **owned** the home for five years. The use test can be met during different periods. However, both tests must be met during the five year period ending on the date of settlement for the sale of the principal residence. You do not have to be living in the property when it is sold. It is important to recognize that the **gain is excluded** – not deferred – and you do not have to purchase a replacement property. You may even convert one of your rental properties into your new principal residence and start a new two year period.

An **exception** to the ownership test, is that if you received the property in a 1031 exchange, it must be **owned for five years** if the exclusion is to be claimed. Congress added §121(d)(10) in 2004 to add the five year ownership period requirement **only** if the principal residence was received in a 1031 exchange. Some text in Pub. 523 may imply that the exclusion cannot be taken if property was received in a like-kind exchange. This is not correct. The exclusion may be taken.

When you **sell** your main home, gain not excluded is any **depreciation** you took on the property after May 6, 1997. For instance if the house was rented, all the Section 1250 depreciation, properly called 'Unrecaptured Section 1250 Gain', will be recaptured.

5. Non-Qualified Use.

Also, regardless of how you obtained the property, if it was rented out after January 1, 2009 and before it was converted to your main home, you must account for the **"non-qualified use"** period gain when you sell the property later as your principal residence. The percent of gain that cannot be claimed as an exclusion is figured as follows: the days the residence was not your main home after December 31, 2008 divided by the <u>total days of your ownership</u> will give you a percentage to the third place.

This percentage is multiplied against the gain on the sale, **less depreciation**, to provide what dollar amount of the exclusion cannot be claimed. IRS Publication 523 and Worksheet #2 therein, fully explains non-qualified use. Thankfully, there are included a number of exceptions shown as to when the non-qualified use period is never considered or excluded.

To get all the details and some worksheets to figure §121 exclusion go to IRS Pub 523 "Selling Your Home".

6. **Suspension of Five-Year Period.** IRC Section 121 was amended to suspend for a maximum of ten years the running of the five year period while the taxpayer or their spouse is "serving on qualified official extended duty". Originally the suspension applied to military personnel and Foreign Service members. It has been expanded to include certain members of the Peace Corps and intelligence community. For example: A military member lives in his personal residence and then gets orders sending them to school and overseas for seven years. They rent out the house while they are gone. Then they wish to sell the property. When sold they can still claim the exclusion, because with the suspension, they have lived in the house for two of the last five years.

7. **Combining Sections 121 and 1031.** Often a sale will include both a business property and a principal residence. A farm along with the family farm house is good example of such a situation. This provision was covered in Paragraph 4 of Chapter 13.

Chapter 19

FINAL SUMMARY

1. **Prior Chapters.** The chapters prior to this final chapter explained the basic 1031 rules and the many situations that a 1031 exchange can involve. Also explained was the possible tax impact if the property was sold instead of doing a 1031 exchange, and what the reinvestment rules are for full or partial tax deferral.

2. **Basic Reinvestment.** In addition to the requirement to exchange like-kind real property for like-kind property (real estate for real estate), investors often think they only have to buy a replacement property equal to or greater than their proceeds from the relinquished property. This is wrong thinking.

The reinvestment rules listed in Chapter 5 provide the guidance for reinvestment necessary to achieve 100% deferment of all taxes. These important basic reinvestment rules are:

> **Rule 1** - Replacement property(ies) must have an equal or greater acquisition cost then the adjusted selling price of the relinquished property(ies).

> **Rule 2 -** All the procees/cash received from the transfer of the relinquished property must be reinvested.

> **Rule 3 -** Replacement property should have a new or assumed mortgage total that is equal to or greater than the debt paid off on the relinquished property – **or the exchanger must add new cash to offset the difference.**

> **Rule 4 -** Exchanger should not receive non-like property – including owner held notes, cash or personal property.

3. **Critical Rules.** This chapter is also a summary of the **critical** rules and **warnings** that must be followed for a 1031 exchange to qualify. The critical rules to follow are as follows:

   a. An **'exchange agreement'** must **exist and be signed** by the exchanger and qualified intermediary (QI) **prior** to settlement of the first relinquished property (this also hires the QI).

b. The relinquished property contract must be **assigned** to the QI, and all parties to the contract must be **notified** of the assignment, **prior** to the settlement of the relinquished property.

c. At settlement the 'exchange escrow funds' (normally all the proceeds) are **sent direct to the QI** by settlement agent. The exchanger may not receive, or touch any of the 'exchange escrow funds'.

d. **Identify** replacement property (normally to QI) in written document, **signed** by exchanger, by **45 days of settlement of relinquished property.** Identification should be unambiguous, and follow one of following three rules:

(1) Three (3) Property rule – can be of any value (most popular)

(2) 200% rule – if more than 3 properties are identified, list value cannot exceed 200% of value of what was relinquished.

(3) 95% rule – if 4 or more properties are identified, and list exceeds 200% of value of relinquished property, 95% of identified property must be bought.

If buying only a percentage of identified property – the percentage should be listed.

e. Copy of all replacement property contracts are **sent** to QI, and exchanger's rights in contract are **assigned** to QI, and all parties to the contract are provided written **notification** of the assignment.

f. Within 180 days of transfer of first relinquished property, exchanger must **receive** (settle on) replacement property.

g. At end of exchange period, QI provides any remaining escrow funds and any interest earned to the exchanger.

h. Exchanger files IRS form 8824 with normal income tax return for the tax year in which first relinquished property was transferred.

4. Warnings.

1) **Release of Funds.** The QI **may not release funds**, until contract is assigned, until end of 45th day if no ID submitted, or until all identified property is purchased, or after the end of the 180-day exchange period or due date (with on-time extension) of tax return. **If funds are released early - the 1031 exchange may be invalid.**

2) **Improvements after settlement**. All desired improvements should be part of initial purchase. 1031 funds cannot be used for **improvements** after exchanger owns the property.

3) **Disbursements.** Cash disbursements **(including deposits) can** only be made from money in escrow account **after** contract is assigned to QI. QI **can**

not give exchanger escrow money directly once exchange has started – only when it has ended. Only third party (like settlement agent) can **disburse** any funds to exchanger.

4) **Loan Size.** *Careful.* The mortgage(s) obtained should not be so high that the exchanger does not have to invest all the cash received.

5) **Adjustments.** To avoid taxable boot, **rent and security deposit adjustments** should be made outside of closing.

6) **Related Person.** A related person may buy relinquished property. **Avoid** purchase of new replacement property from a **related person**, unless they also are doing a 1031 exchange of the property.

7) **Same Taxpayer.** To exchange a property, exchanger must be an owner and on title (except DST) for all properties. The person(s)/entity exchanging relinquished property must be the same person(s)/entity (or a disregarded entity - like a single member LLC, or revocable living trust) **on contract for replacement property**. The SAME owner(s) (or their disregarded entity) must exchange all properties. *Simple check:* The SSAN or EIN must belong to the same taxpayer for all exchange properties.

8) **After 45th Day - No ID Changes.** After the 45th day, identification list **cannot be changed**.

9) **180 Days Total**. You must go to settlement on all desired replacement property by end of **180 day exchange period** (180 days includes the 45 day identification period) or due date of return.

When in doubt about requirements – call your QI or tax advisor.

5. Exchange Checklist. An exchange checklist is available in the Appendix. It is recommended this checklist be used to ensure all the necessary steps are taken.

APPENDICES

APPENDIX A
IRC § 1031 –Exchange of Real Property Held for Productive Use or Investment.

APPENDIX B
IRS Regulation §1.1031(k) -1
Treatment of Tax Deferred Exchanges

APPENDIX C
Revenue Procedure 2000-37 (Reverse Exchange)
Revenue Procedure 2008-16 (Vacation Home Safe Harbor)
IRS Form 1040 – Schedule E
Exchange Checklist

APPENDIX A

26 U.S. Code § 1031.Exchange of Real Property Held for Productive Use or Investment

(a)NONRECOGNITION OF GAIN OR LOSS FROM EXCHANGES SOLELY IN KIND

(1)IN GENERAL

No gain or loss shall be recognized on the exchange of real property held for productive use in a trade or business or for investment if such real property is exchanged solely for real property of like kind which is to be held either for productive use in a trade or business or for investment.

(2)EXCEPTION FOR REAL PROPERTY HELD FOR SALE

This subsection shall not apply to any exchange of real property held primarily for sale.

(3)REQUIREMENT THAT PROPERTY BE IDENTIFIED AND THAT EXCHANGE BE COMPLETED NOT MORE THAN **180** DAYS AFTER TRANSFER OF EXCHANGED PROPERTY

For purposes of this subsection, any property received by the taxpayer shall be treated as property which is not like-kind property if—

(A) such property is not identified as property to be received in the exchange on or before the day which is 45 days after the date on which the taxpayer transfers the property relinquished in the exchange, or

(B) such property is received after the earlier of—

(i)the day which is 180 days after the date on which the taxpayer transfers the property relinquished in the exchange, or

(ii)
the due date (determined with regard to extension) for the transferor's return of the tax imposed by this chapter for the taxable year in which the transfer of the relinquished property occurs.

(b)Gain from exchanges not solely in kind

If an exchange would be within the provisions of subsection (a), of section 1035(a), of section 1036(a), or of section 1037(a), if it were not for the fact that the property received in exchange consists not only of property permitted by such provisions to be received without the recognition of gain, but also of other property or money, then the gain, if any, to the recipient shall be recognized, but in an amount not in excess of the sum of such money and the fair market value of such other property.

(c)Loss from exchanges not solely in kind

If an exchange would be within the provisions of subsection (a), of section 1035(a), of section 1036(a), or of section 1037(a), if it were not for the fact that the property received in exchange consists not only of property permitted by such provisions to be received without the recognition of gain or loss, but also of other property or money, then no loss from the exchange shall be recognized.

(d)Basis

If property was acquired on an exchange described in this section, section 1035(a), section 1036(a), or section 1037(a), then the basis shall be the same as that of the property exchanged, decreased in the amount of any money received by the taxpayer and increased in the amount of gain or decreased in the amount of loss to the taxpayer that was recognized on such exchange. If the property so acquired consisted in part of the type of property permitted by this section, section 1035(a), section 1036(a), or section 1037(a), to be received without the recognition of gain or loss, and in part of other property, the basis provided in this subsection shall be allocated between the properties (other than money) received, and for the purpose of the allocation there shall be assigned to such other property an amount equivalent to its fair market value at the date of the exchange. For purposes of this section, section 1035(a), and section 1036(a), where as part of the consideration to the taxpayer another party to the exchange assumed (as determined under section 357(d)) a liability of the taxpayer, such assumption shall be considered as money received by the taxpayer on the exchange.

(e)Application to certain partnerships

For purposes of this section, an interest in a partnership which has in effect a valid election under section 761(a) to be excluded from the application of all of subchapter K shall be treated as an interest in each of the assets of such partnership and not as an interest in a partnership.

(f)SPECIAL RULES FOR EXCHANGES BETWEEN RELATED PERSONS

(1)IN GENERAL If—

(A)

a taxpayer exchanges property with a <u>related person</u>,

(B)

there is nonrecognition of gain or loss to the taxpayer under this section with respect to the exchange of such property (determined without regard to this subsection), and

(C)before the date 2 years after the date of the last transfer which was part of such exchange—

(i)

the <u>related person</u> disposes of such property, or

(ii)

the taxpayer disposes of the property received in the exchange from the <u>related person</u> which was of like kind to the property transferred by the taxpayer,

there shall be no nonrecognition of gain or loss under this section to the taxpayer with respect to such exchange; except that any gain or loss recognized by the taxpayer by reason of this subsection shall be taken into account as of the date on which the <u>disposition</u> referred to in subparagraph (C) occurs.

(2)CERTAIN DISPOSITIONS NOT TAKEN INTO ACCOUNT For purposes of paragraph (1) (C), there shall not be taken into account any <u>disposition</u>—

(A)

after the earlier of the death of the taxpayer or the death of the <u>related person</u>,

(B)

in a compulsory or involuntary conversion (within the meaning of <u>section 1033</u>) if the exchange occurred before the threat or imminence of such conversion, or

(C)

with respect to which it is established to the satisfaction of the Secretary that neither the exchange nor such <u>disposition</u> had as one of its principal purposes the avoidance of Federal income tax.

(3) RELATED PERSON

For purposes of this subsection, the term "<u>related person</u>" means any person bearing a relationship to the taxpayer described in <u>section 267(b)</u> or 707(b)(1).

(4) TREATMENT OF CERTAIN TRANSACTIONS

This section shall not apply to any exchange which is part of a transaction (or series of transactions) structured to avoid the purposes of this subsection.

(g) SPECIAL RULE WHERE SUBSTANTIAL DIMINUTION OF RISK

(1) IN GENERAL

If paragraph (2) applies to any property for any period, the running of the period set forth in subsection (f)(1)(C) with respect to such property shall be suspended during such period.

(2) PROPERTY TO WHICH SUBSECTION APPLIES This paragraph shall apply to any property for any period during which the holder's risk of loss with respect to the property is substantially diminished by—

(A)

the holding of a put with respect to such property,

(B)

the holding by another person of a right to acquire such property, or

(C)

a short sale or any other transaction.

(h) SPECIAL RULES FOR FOREIGN REAL PROPERTY

Real property located in the United States and real property located outside the United States are not property of a like kind.

APPENDIX B

26 CFR § 1.1031(k)-1 - Treatment of Deferred Exchanges.

§ 1.1031(k)-1 <u>Treatment</u> of deferred exchanges.

(a) *Overview.* This section provides <u>rules</u> for the <u>application</u> of section 1031 and the regulations thereunder in the case of a "deferred <u>exchange</u>." For <u>purposes</u> of section 1031 and this section, a deferred <u>exchange</u> is <u>defined</u> as an <u>exchange</u> in which, pursuant to an <u>agreement</u>, the <u>taxpayer</u> transfers <u>property</u> held for productive use in a <u>trade or business</u> or for <u>investment</u> (the "relinquished property") and subsequently receives <u>property</u> to be held either for productive use in a <u>trade or business</u> or for <u>investment</u> (the "replacement property"). In the case of a deferred <u>exchange</u>, if the <u>requirements</u> set forth in paragraphs <u>(b)</u>, <u>(c)</u>, and <u>(d)</u> of this section (relating to <u>identification</u> and <u>receipt</u> of replacement property) are not satisfied, the replacement <u>property</u> received by the <u>taxpayer</u> will be treated as <u>property</u> which is not of a like kind to the relinquished <u>property</u>. In order to constitute a deferred <u>exchange</u>, the transaction must be an <u>exchange</u> (i.e., a <u>transfer of property</u> for <u>property</u>, as distinguished from a <u>transfer of property</u> for money). For <u>example</u>, a sale of <u>property</u> followed by a <u>purchase</u> of <u>property</u> of a like kind does not qualify for nonrecognition of <u>gain or loss</u> under section 1031 regardless of whether the <u>identification</u> and <u>receipt</u> <u>requirements</u> of section 1031(a)(3) and paragraphs <u>(b)</u>, <u>(c)</u>, and <u>(d)</u> of this section are satisfied. The <u>transfer</u> of relinquished <u>property</u> in a deferred <u>exchange</u> is not within the provisions of section 1031(a) if, as part of the consideration, the <u>taxpayer</u> receives money or <u>property</u> which does not meet the <u>requirements</u> of section 1031(a), but the <u>transfer</u>, if otherwise qualified, will be within the provisions of either section 1031 <u>(b)</u> or <u>(c)</u>. See § 1.1031(a)-1(a)(2). In addition, in the case of a <u>transfer</u> of relinquished <u>property</u> in a deferred <u>exchange</u>, <u>gain or loss</u> may be recognized if the <u>taxpayer</u> actually or constructively receives money or <u>property</u> which does not meet the <u>requirements</u> of section 1031(a) before the <u>taxpayer</u> actually receives like-kind replacement <u>property</u>. If the <u>taxpayer</u> actually or constructively receives money or <u>property</u> which does not meet the <u>requirements</u> of section 1031(a) in the full <u>amount</u> of the consideration for the relinquished <u>property</u>, the transaction will constitute a sale, and not a deferred <u>exchange</u>, even though the <u>taxpayer</u> may ultimately receive like-kind replacement <u>property</u>. For <u>purposes</u> of this section, <u>property</u> which does not meet the <u>requirements</u> of section 1031(a) (whether by being described in section 1031(a)(2) or otherwise) is referred to as "other <u>property</u>." For <u>rules</u> regarding actual and constructive <u>receipt</u>, and <u>safe harbors</u> therefrom, see paragraphs <u>(f)</u> and <u>(g)</u>, respectively, of this section. For <u>rules</u> regarding the determination of gain or loss recognized and the basis of property received in a deferred exchange, see paragraph (j) of this section.

(b) *Identification and receipt requirements -*
   (1) *In general.* In the case of a deferred exchange, any replacement property received by the taxpayer will be treated as property which is not of a like kind to the relinquished property if -

   (i) The replacement property is not "identified" before the end of the "identification period," or

   (ii) The identified replacement property is not received before the end of the "exchange period."

(2) *Identification period and exchange period.*

   (i) The identification period begins on the date the taxpayer transfers the relinquished property and ends at midnight on the 45th day thereafter.

   (ii) The exchange period begins on the date the taxpayer transfers the relinquished property and ends at midnight on the earlier of the 180th day thereafter or the due date (including extensions) for the taxpayer's return of the tax imposed by chapter 1 of subtitle A of the Code for the taxable year in which the transfer of the relinquished property occurs.

   (iii) If, as part of the same deferred exchange, the taxpayer transfers more than one relinquished property and the relinquished properties are transferred on different dates, the identification period and the exchange period are determined by reference to the earliest date on which any of the properties are transferred.

   (iv) For purposes of this paragraph (b)(2), property is transferred when the property is disposed of within the meaning of section 1001(a).

(3) *Example.* This paragraph (b) may be illustrated by the following example.

EXAMPLE:

(i) M is a corporation that files its Federal income tax return on a calendar year basis. M and C enter into an agreement for an exchange of property that requires M to transfer property X to C. Under the agreement, M is to identify like-kind replacement property which C is required to purchase and to transfer to M. M transfers property X to C on November 16, 1992.

(ii) The identification period ends at midnight on December 31, 1992, the day which is 45 days after the date of transfer of property X. The exchange period ends at midnight on March 15, 1993, the due date for M's Federal income tax return for the taxable year in which M transferred property X. However, if M is allowed the automatic six-month extension for filing its tax return, the exchange period ends at midnight on May 15, 1993, the day which is 180 days after the date of transfer of property X.

(c) *Identification of replacement property before the end of the identification period* -

(1) *In general.* For purposes of paragraph (b)(1)(i) of this section (relating to the identification requirement), replacement property is identified before the end of the identification period only if the requirements of this paragraph (c) are satisfied with respect to the replacement property. However, any replacement property that is received by the taxpayer before the end of the identification period will in all events be treated as identified before the end of the identification period.

(2) *Manner of identifying replacement property.* Replacement property is identified only if it is designated as replacement property in a written document signed by the taxpayer and hand delivered, mailed, telecopied, or otherwise sent before the end of the identification period to either -

(i) The person obligated to transfer the replacement property to the taxpayer (regardless of whether that person is a disqualified person as defined in paragraph (k) of this section); or

(ii) Any other person involved in the exchange other than the taxpayer or a disqualified person (as defined in paragraph (k) of this section).

Examples of persons involved in the exchange include any of the parties to the exchange, an intermediary, an escrow agent, and a title company. An identification of replacement property made in a written agreement for the exchange of properties signed by all parties thereto before the end of the identification period will be treated as satisfying the requirements of this paragraph (c)(2).

(3) *Description of replacement property.* Replacement property is identified only if it is unambiguously described in the written document or agreement. Real property generally is unambiguously described if it is described by a legal description, street address, or distinguishable name (e.g., the Mayfair Apartment Building). Personal property generally is unambiguously described if it is described by a specific description of the particular type of property. For example, a truck generally is unambigously described if it is described by a specific make, model, and year.

(4) *Alternative and multiple properties.*

(i) The taxpayer may identify more than one replacement property. Regardless of the number of relinguished properties transferred by the taxpayer as part of the same deferred exchange, the maximum number of replacement properties that the taxpayer may identify is -

(A) Three properties without regard to the fair market values of the properties (the "3-property rule"), or

(B) Any number of properties as long as their aggregate fair market value as of the end of the identification period does not exceed 200 percent of the aggregate fair market value of all the relinguished properties as of the date the relinguished properties were transferred by the taxpayer (the "200-percent rule").

(ii) If, as of the end of the identification period, the taxpayer has identified more properties as replacement properties than permitted by paragraph (c) (4)(i) of this section, the taxpayer is treated as if no replacement property had been identified. The preceding sentence will not apply, however, and an identification satisfying the requirements of paragraph (c)(4)(i) of this section will be considered made, with respect to -

(A) Any replacement property received by the taxpayer before the end of the identification period, and

(B) Any replacement property identified before the end of the identification period and received before the end of the exchange period, but only if the taxpayer receives before the end of the exchange period identified replacement property the fair market vlaue of which is at least 95 percent of the aggregate fair market value of all identified replacement properties (the "95-percent rule").

For this purpose, the fair market value of each identified replacement property is determined as of the earlier of the date the property is received by the taxpayer or the last day of the exchange period.

(iii) For purposes of applying the 3-property rule, the 200-percent rule, and the 95-percent rule, all identifications of replacement property, other than identifications of replacement property that have been revoked in the manner provided in paragraph (c)(6) of this section, are taken into account.

For *example*, if, in a deferred *exchange*, B transfers *property* X with a *fair market value* of $100,000 to C and B receives like-kind *property* Y with a *fair market value* of $50,000 before the end of the *identification* period, under *paragraph (c)(1)* of this section, *property* Y is treated as identified *by reason of* being received before the end of the *identification* period. Thus, under *paragraph (c)(4)(i)* of this section, B may identify either two additional replacement properties of any *fair market value* or any number of additional replacement properties as long as the aggregate *fair market value* of the additional replacement properties does not exceed $150,000.

(5) *Incidental property disregarded.*

(i) Solely for *purposes* of applying this paragraph *(c)*, *property* that is incidental to a larger item of *property* is not treated as *property* that is separate from the larger item of *property*. *Property* is incidental to a larger item of *property* if -

(A) In standard commercial transactions, the *property* is typically *transferred* together with the larger item of *property*, and

(B) The aggregate *fair market value* of all of the incidental *property* does not exceed 15 percent of the aggregate *fair market value* of the larger item of *property*.

(ii) This paragraph (c)(5) may be illustrated by the following *examples*.

EXAMPLE 1.

For purposes of *paragraph (c)* of this section, a spare tire and tool kit will not be treated as separate property from a truck with a fair market value of $10,000, if the aggregate fair market value of the spare tire and tool kit does not exceed $1,500. For purposes of the 3-property rule, the truck, spare tire, and tool kit are treated as 1 property. Moreover, for purposes of *paragraph (c)(3)* of this section (relating to the description of replacement property), the truck, spare tire, and tool kit are all considered to be unambiguously described if the make, model, and year of the truck are specified, even if no reference is made to the spare tire and tool kit.

EXAMPLE 2.

For purposes of *paragraph (c)* of this section, furniture, laundry machines, and other miscellaneous items of personal property will not be treated as separate property from an apartment building with a fair market value of $1,000,000, if the aggregate fair market value of the furniture, laundry machines, and other personal property does not exceed $150,000. For purposes of the 3-property rule, the apartment building, furniture, laundry machines, and other personal property are treated as 1 property. Moreover, for purposes of paragraph (c)(3) of this section (relating to the description of replacement property), the apartment building, furniture, laundry machines, and other personal property are all considered to be unambiguously described if the legal description, street address, or distinguishable name of the apartment building is specified, even if no reference is made to the furniture, laundry machines, and other personal property.

(6) ***Revocation of identification.*** An identification of replacement property may be revoked at any time before the end of the identification period. An identification of replacement property is revoked only if the revocation is made in a written document signed by the taxpayer and hand delivered, mailed, telecopied, or otehwise sent before the end of the identification period to the person to whom the identification of the replacement property was sent. An identification of replacement property that is made in a written agreement for the exchange of properties is treated as revoked only if the revocation is made in a written amendment to the agreement or in a written document signed by the taxpayer and hand delivered, mailed, telecopied, or otehwise sent before the end of the identification period to all of the parties to the agreement.

(7) ***Examples.*** This paragraph (c) may be illustrated by the following examples. Unless otherwise provided in an example, the following facts are assumed: B, a calendar year taxpayer, and C agree to enter into a deferred exchange. Pursuant to their agreement, B transfers real property X to C on May 17, 1991. Real property X, which has been held by B for investment, is unencumbered and has a fair market value on May 17, 1991, of $100,000. On or before July 1, 1991 (the end of the identification period), B is to identify replacement property that is of a like kind to real property X. On or before November 13, 1991 (the end of the exchange period), C is required to purchase the property identified by B and to transfer that property to B. To the extent the fair market value of the replacement property transferred to B is greater or less than the fair market value of real property X, either B or C, as applicable, will make up the difference by paying cash to the other party after the date the replacement property is received by B. No replacement property is identified in the agreement. When subsequently identified, the replacement property is described by legal description and is of a like kind to real property X (determined without regard to section 1031(a)(3) and this section). B intends to hold the replacement property received for investment.

EXAMPLE 1.

(i) On July 2, 1991, B identifies real property E as replacement property by designating real property E as replacement property in a written document signed by B and personally delivered to C.

102

(ii) Because the <u>identification</u> was made after the end of the <u>identification</u> period, pursuant to <u>paragraph (b)(1)(i)</u> of this section (relating to the <u>identification</u> requirement), <u>real property</u> E is treated as <u>property</u> which is not of a like kind to <u>real property</u> X.

EXAMPLE 2.

(i) C is a corporation of which 20 percent of the outstanding stock is owned by B. On July 1, 1991, B identifies real property F as replacement property by designating real property F as replacement property in a written document signed by B and mailed to C.

(ii) Because C is the <u>person</u> obligated to <u>transfer</u> the replacement <u>property</u> to B, <u>real property</u> F is identified before the end of the <u>identification</u> period. The fact that C is a "disqualified person" as <u>defined</u> in <u>paragraph (k)</u> of this section does not change this <u>result</u>.

(iii) <u>Real property</u> F would also have been treated as identified before the end of the <u>identification</u> period if, instead of sending the <u>identification</u> to C, B had designated <u>real property</u> F as replacement <u>property</u> in a <u>written agreement</u> for the <u>exchange</u> of properties signed by all parties thereto on or before July 1, 1991.

EXAMPLE 3.

(i) On June 3, 1991, B identifies the replacement property as "unimproved land located in Hood County with a fair market value not to exceed $100,000." The designation is made in a written document signed by B and personally delivered to C. On July 8, 1991, B and C agree that real property G is the property described in the June 3, 1991 document.

(ii) Because <u>real property</u> G was not unambiguously described before the end of the <u>identification</u> period, no replacement <u>property</u> is identified before the end of the <u>identification</u> period.

EXAMPLE 4.

(i) On June 28, 1991, B identifies real properties H, J, and K as replacement properties by designating these properties as replacement properties in a written document signed by B and personally delivered to C. The written document provides that by August 1, 1991, B will orally inform C which of the identified properties C is to transfer to B. As of July 1, 1991, the fair market values of real properties H, J, and K are $75,000, $100,000, and $125,000, respectively.

(ii) Because B did not identify more than three properties as replacement properties, the <u>requirements</u> of the 3-property <u>rule</u> are satisfied, and real properties H, J, and K are all identified before the end of the <u>identification</u> period.

EXAMPLE 5.

(i) On May 17, 1991, B identifies real properties L, M, N, and P as replacement properties by designating these properties as replacement properties in a written document signed by B and personally delivered to C. The written document provides that by July 2, 1991, B will orally inform C which of the identified properties C is to transfer to B. As of July 1, 1991, the fair market values of real properties L, M, N, and P are $30,000, $40,000, $50,000, and $60,000, respectively.

(ii) Although B identified more than three properties as replacement properties, the aggregate <u>fair market value</u> of the identified properties as of the end of the <u>identification</u> period ($180,000) did not exceed 200 percent of the aggregate <u>fair market value</u> of <u>real property</u> X (200% × $100,000 = $200,000). Therefore, the <u>requirements</u> of the 200-percent <u>rule</u> are satisfied, and real properties L, M, N, and P are all identified before the end of the <u>identification</u> period.

EXAMPLE 6.

(i) On June 21, 1991, B identifies real properties Q, R, and S as replacement properties by designating these properties as replacement properties in a written document signed by B and mailed to C. On June 24, 1991, B identifies real properties T and U as replacement properties in a written document signed by B and mailed to C. On June 28, 1991, B revokes the identification of real properties Q and R in a written document signed by B and personally delivered to C.

(ii) B has revoked the <u>identification</u> of real properties Q and R in the manner provided by <u>paragraph (c)(6)</u> of this section. <u>Identifications</u> of replacement <u>property</u> that have been revoked in the manner provided by <u>paragraph (c)</u> <u>(6)</u> of this section are not taken into <u>account</u> for <u>purposes</u> of applying the 3-property <u>rule</u>. Thus, as of June 28, 1991, B has identified only replacement properties S, T, and U for <u>purposes</u> of the 3-property <u>rule</u>. Because B did not identify more than three properties as replacement properties for <u>purposes</u> of the 3-property <u>rule</u>, the <u>requirements</u> of that <u>rule</u> are satisfied, and real properties S, T, and U are all identified before the end of the <u>identification</u> period.

EXAMPLE 7.

(i) On May 20, 1991, B identifies real properties V and W as replacement properties by designating these properties as replacement properties in a written document signed by B and personally delivered to C. On June 4, 1991, B identifies real properties Y and Z as replacement properties in the same manner. On June 5, 1991, B telephones C and orally revokes the identification of real properties V and W. As of July 1, 1991, the fair market values of real properties V, W, Y, and Z are $50,000, $70,000, $90,000, and $100,000, respectively. On July 31, 1991, C purchases real property Y and Z and transfers them to B.

(ii) Pursuant to paragraph (c)(6) of this section (relating to revocation of identification), the oral revocation of the identification of real properties V and W is invalid. Thus, the identification of real properties V and W is taken into account for purposes of determining whether the requirements of paragraph (c)(4) of this section (relating to the identification of alternative and multiple properties) are satisfied. Because B identified more than three properties and the aggregate fair market value of the identified properties as of the end of the identification period ($310,000) exceeds 200 percent of the fair market value of real property X (200% × $100,000 = $200,000), the requirements of paragraph (c)(4) of this section are not satisfied, and B is treated as if B did not identify any replacement property.

(d) *Receipt of identified replacement property -*

(1) *In general.* For purposes of paragraph (b)(1)(ii) of this section (relating to the receipt requirement), the identified replacement property is received before the end of the exchange period only if the requriements of this paragraph (d) are satisfied with respect to the replacement property. In the case of a deferred exchange, the identified replacement property is received before the end of the exchange period if -

(i) The taxpayer receives the replacement property before the end of the exchange period, and

(ii) The replacement property received is substantially the same property as identified.

If the taxpayer has identified more than one replacement property, section 1031(a)(3)(B) and this paragraph (d) are applied separately to each replacement property.

(2) *Examples.* This paragraph (d) may be illustrated by the following examples. The following facts are assumed: B, a calendar year taxpayer, and C agree to enter

into a deferred exchange. Pursuant to their agreement, B transfers real property X to C on May 17, 1991. Real property X, which has been held by B for investment, is unencumbered and has a fair market value on May 17, 1991, of $100,000. On or before July 1, 1991 (the end of the identification period), B is to identify replacement property that is of a like kind to real property X. On or before November 13, 1991 (the end of the exchange period), C is required to purchase the property identified by B and to transfer that property to B. To the extent the fair market value of the replacement property transferred to B is greater or less than the fair market value of real property X, either B or C, as applicable, will make up the difference by paying cash to the other party after the date the replacement property is received by B. The replacement property is identified in a manner that satisfies paragraph (c) of this section (relating to identification of replacement property) and is of a like kind to real property X (determined without regard to section 1031(a)(3) and this section). B intends to hold any replacement property received for investment.

EXAMPLE 1.

(i) In the agreement, B identifies real properties J, K, and L as replacement properties. The agreement provides that by July 26, 1991, B will orally inform C which of the properties C is to transfer to B.

(ii) As of July 1, 1991, the fair market values of real properties J, K, and L are $75,000, $100,000, and $125,000, respectively. On July 26, 1991, B instructs C to acquire real property K. On October 31, 1991, C purchases real property K for $100,000 and transfers the property to B.

(iii) Because real property K was identified before the end of the identification period and was received before the end of the exchange period, the identification and receipt requirements of section 1031(a)(3) and this section are satisfied with respect to real property K.

EXAMPLE 2.

(i) In the agreement, B identifies real property P as replacement property. Real property P consists of two acres of unimproved land. On October 15, 1991, the owner of real property P erects a fence on the property. On November 1, 1991, C purchases real property P and transfers it to B.

(ii) The erection of the fence on real property P subsequent to its identification did not alter the basic nature or character of real property P as unimproved land. B is considered to have received substantially the same property as identified.

EXAMPLE 3.

(i) In the agreement, B identifies real property Q as replacement property. Real property Q consists of a barn on two acres of land and has a fair market value of $250,000 ($187,500 for the barn and underlying land and $87,500 for the remaining land). As of July 26, 1991, real property Q remains unchanged and has a fair market value of $250,000. On that date, at B's direction, C purchases the barn and underlying land for $187,500 and transfers it to B, and B pays $87,500 to C.

(ii) The barn and underlying land differ in basic nature or character from real property Q as a whole, B is not considered to have received substantially the same property as identified.

EXAMPLE 4.

(i) In the agreement, B identifies real property R as replacement property. Real property R consists of two acres of unimproved land and has a fair market value of $250,000. As of October 3, 1991, real property R remains unimproved and has a fair market value of $250,000. On that date, at B's direction, C purchases 1 1/2 acres of real property R for $187,500 and transfers it to B, and B pays $87,500 to C.

(ii) The portion of real property R that B received does not differ from the basic nature or character of real property R as a whole. Moreover, the fair market value of the portion of real property R that B received ($187,500) is 75 percent of the fair market value of real property R as of the date of receipt. Accordingly, B is considered to have received substantially the same property as identified.

(e) *Special rules for identification and receipt of replacement property to be produced* -

(1) *In general.* A transfer of relinquished property in a deferred exchange will not fail to qualify for nonrecognition of gain or loss under section 1031 merely because the replacement property is not in existence or is being produced at the time the property is identified as replacement property. For purposes of this paragraph (e), the terms "produced" and "production" have the same meanings as provided in section 263A(g)(1) and the regulations thereunder.

(2) *Identification of replacement property to be produced.*

(i) In the case of replacement property that is to be produced, the replacement property must be identified as provided in paragraph (c) of this section (relating to identification of replacement property). For example, if the identified replacement property consists of improved real property where the improvements are to be constructed, the description of the replacement property satisfies the requirements of paragraph (c)(3) of this section (relating to description of replacement property) if a legal description is provided for the underlying land and as much detail is provided regarding construction of the improvements as is practicable at the time the identification is made.

(ii) For purposes of paragraphs (c)(4)(i)(B) and (c)(5) of this section (relating to the 200-percent rule and incidental property), the fair market value of replacement property that is to be produced is its estimated fair market value as of the date it is expected to be received by the taxpayer.

(3) *Receipt of replacement property to be produced.*

(i) For purposes of paragraph (d)(1)(ii) of this section (relating to receipt of the identified replacement property), in determining whether the replacement property received by the taxpayer is substantially the same property as identified where the identified replacement property is property to be produced, variations due to usual or typical production changes are not taken into account. However, if substantial changes are made in the property to be produced, the replacement property received will not be considered to be substantially the same property as identified.

(ii) If the identified replacement property is personal property to be produced, the replacement property received will not be considered to be substantially the same property as identified unless production of the replacement property received is completed on or before the date the property is received by the taxpayer.

(iii) If the identified replacement property is real property to be produced and the production of the property is not completed on or before the date the taxpayer receives the property, the property received will be considered to be substantially the same property as identified only if, had production been completed on or before the date the taxpayer receives the replacement property, the property received would have been considered to be substantially the same property as identified. Even so, the property received is considered to be substantially the same property as identified only to the extent the property received constitutes real property under local law.

(4) *Additional rules.* The transfer of relinquished property is not within the provisions of section 1031(a) if the relinquished property is transferred in exchange for services (including production services). Thus, any additional production occurring with respect to the replacement property after the property is received by the taxpayer will not be treated as the receipt of property of a like kind.

(5) *Example.* This paragraph (e) may be illustrated by the following example.

EXAMPLE:

(i) B, a calendar year taxpayer, and C agree to enter into a deferred exchange. Pursuant to their agreement, B transfers improved real property X and personal property Y to C on May 17, 1991. On or before November 13, 1991 (the end of the exchange period), C is required to transfer to B real property M, on which C is constructing improvements, and personal property N, which C is producing. C is obligated to complete the improvements and production regardless of when properties M and N are transferred to B. Properties M and N are identified in a manner that satisfies paragraphs (c) (relating to identification of replacement property) and (e)(2) of this section. In addition, properties M and N are of a like kind, respectively, to real property X and personal property Y (determined without regard to section 1031(a)(3) and this section). On November 13, 1991, when construction of the improvements to property M is 20 percent completed and the production of property N is 90 percent completed, C transfers to B property M and property N. If construction of the improvements had been completed, property M would have been considered to be substantially the same property as identified. Under local law, property M constitutes real property to the extent of the underlying land and the 20 percent of the construction that is completed.

(ii) Because property N is personal property to be produced and production of property N is not completed before the date the property is received by B, property N is not considered to be substantially the same property as identified and is treated as property which is not of a like kind to property Y.

(iii) Property M is considered to be substantially the same property as identified to the extent of the underlying land and the 20 percent of the construction that is completed when property M is received by B. However, any additional construction performed by C with respect to property M after November 13, 1991, is not treated as the receipt of property of a like kind.

(f) *Receipt of money or other property* -

(1) *In general.* A transfer of relinquished property in a deferred exchange is not within the provisions of section 1031(a) if, as part of the consideration, the taxpayer receives money or other property. However, such a transfer, if otherwise qualified, will be within the provisions of either section 1031 (b) or (c). See § 1.1031(a)-1(a) (2). In addition, in the case of a transfer of relinquished property in a deferred exchange, gain or loss may be recognized if the taxpayer actually or constructively receives money or other property before the taxpayer actually receives like-kind replacement property. If the taxpayer actually or constructively receives money or

109

other property in the full amount of the consideration for the relinquished property before the taxpayer actually receives like-kind replacement property, the transaction will constitute a sale and not a deferred exchange, even though the taxpayer may ultimately receive like-kind replacement property.

(2) *Actual and constructive receipt.* Except as provided in paragraph (g) of this section (relating to safe harbors), for purposes of section 1031 and this section, the determination of whether (or the extent to which) the taxpayer is in actual or constructive receipt of money or other property before the taxpayer actually receives like-kind replacement property is made under the general rules concerning actual and constructive receipt and without regard to the taxpayer's method of accounting. The taxpayer is in actual receipt of money or property at the time the taxpayer actually receives the money or property or receives the economic benefit of the money or property. The taxpayer is in constructive receipt of money or property at the time the money or property is credited to the taxpayer's account, set apart for the taxpayer, or otherwise made available so that the taxpayer may draw upon it at any time or so that the taxpayer can draw upon it if notice of intention to draw is given. Although the taxpayer is not in constructive receipt of money or property if the taxpayer's control of its receipt is subject to substantial limitations or restrictions, the taxpayer is in constructive receipt of the money or property at the time the limitations or restrictions lapse, expire, or are waived. In addition, actual or constructive receipt of money or property by an agent of the taxpayer (determined without regard to paragraph (k) of this section) is actual or constructive receipt by the taxpayer.

(3) *Example.* This paragraph (f) may be illustrated by the following example.

EXAMPLE:

(i) B, a calendar year taxpayer, and C agree to enter into a deferred exchange. Pursuant to the agreement, on May 17, 1991, B transfers real property X to C. Real property X, which has been held by B for investment, is unencumbered and has a fair market value on May 17, 1991, of $100,000. On or before July 1, 1991 (the end of the identification period), B is to identify replacement property that is of a like kind to real property X. On or before November 13, 1991 (the end of the exchange period), C is required to purchase the property identified by B and to transfer that property to B. At any time after May 17, 1991, and before C has purchased the replacement property, B has the right, upon notice, to demand that C pay $100,000 in lieu of acquiring and transferring the replacement property. Pursuant to the agreement, B identifies replacement property, and C purchases the replacement property and transfers it to B.

(ii) Under the agreement, B has the unrestricted right to demand the payment of $100,000 as of May 17, 1991. B is therefore in constructive receipt of $100,000 on that date. Because B is in constructive receipt of money in the full amount of the consideration for the relinquished property before B actually receives the like-kind replacement property, the transaction constitutes a sale, and the transfer of real property X does not qualify for nonrecognition of gain or loss under section 1031. B is treated as if B received the $100,000 in consideration for the sale of real property X and then purchased the like-kind replacement property.

(iii) If B's right to demand payment of the $100,000 were subject to a substantial limitation or restriction (e.g., the agreement provided that B had no right to demand payment before November 14, 1991 (the end of the exchange period)), then, for purposes of this section, B would not be in actual or constructive receipt of the money unless (or until) the limitation or restriction lapsed, expired, or was waived.

(g) *Safe harbors* -

(1) *In general.* Paragraphs (g)(2) through (g)(5) of this section set forth four safe harbors the use of which will result in a determination that the taxpayer is not in actual or constructive receipt of money or other property for purposes of section 1031 and this section. More than one safe harbor can be used in the same deferred exchange, but the terms and conditions of each must be separately satisfied. For purposes of the safe harbor rules, the term "taxpayer" does not include a person or entity utilized in a safe harbor (e.g., a qualified intermediary). See paragraph (g)(8), *Example 3(v),* of this section.

(2) *Security or guarantee arrangements.*

(i) In the case of a deferred exchange, the determination of whether the taxpayer is in actual or constructive receipt of money or other property before the taxpayer actually receives like-kind replacement property will be made without regard to the fact that the obligation of the taxpayer's transferee to transfer the replacement property to the taxpayer is or may be secured or guaranteed by one or more of the following -

(A) A mortgage, deed of trust, or other security interest in property (other than cash or a cash equivalent),

(B) A standby letter of credit which satisfies all of the requirements of § 15A.453-1 (b)(3)(iii) and which may not be drawn upon in the absence of a default of the transferee's obligation to transfer like-kind replacement property to the taxpayer, or

(C) A guarantee of a third party.

(ii) Paragraph (g)(2)(i) of this section ceases to apply at the time the taxpayer has an immediate ability or unrestricted right to receive money or other property pursuant to the security or guarantee arrangement.

(3) *Qualified escrow accounts and qualified trusts.*

(i) In the case of a deferred exchange, the determination of whether the taxpayer is in actual or constructive receipt of money or other property before the taxpayer actually receives like-kind replacement property will be made without regard to the fact that the obligation of the taxpayer's transferee to transfer the replacement property to the taxpayer is or may be secured by cash or a cash equivalent if the cash or cash equivalent is held in a qualified escrow account or in a qualified trust.

(ii) A qualified escrow account is an escrow account wherein -

(A) The escrow holder is not the taxpayer or a disqualified person (as defined in paragraph (k) of this section), and

(B) The escrow agreement expressly limits the taxpayer's rights to receive, pledge, borrow, or otherwise obtain the benefits of the cash or cash equivalent held in the escrow account as provided in paragraph (g)(6) of this section.

(iii) A qualified trust is a trust wherein -

(A) The trustee is not the taxpayer or a disqualified person (as defined in paragraph (k) of this section, except that for this purpose the relationship between the taxpayer and the trustee created by the qualified trust will not be considered a relationship under section 267(b)), and

(B) The trust agreement expressly limits the taxpayer's rights to receive, pledge, borrow, or otherwise obtain the benefits of the cash or cash equivalent held by the trustee as provided in paragraph (g)(6) of this section.

(iv) Paragraph (g)(3)(i) of this section ceases to apply at the time the taxpayer has an immediate ability or unrestricted right to receive, pledge, borrow, or otherwise obtain the benefits of the cash or cash equivalent held in the qualified escrow account or qualified trust. Rights conferred upon the taxpayer under state law to terminate or dismiss the escrow holder of a qualified escrow account or the trustee of a qualified trust are disregarded for this purpose.

(v) A taxpayer may receive money or other property directly from a party to the exchange, but not from a qualified escrow account or a qualified trust, without affecting the application of paragraph (g)(3)(i) of this section.

(4) *Qualified intermediaries.*

(i) In the case of a taxpayer's transfer of relinquished property involving a qualified intermediary, the qualified intermediary is not considered the agent of the taxpayer for purposes of section 1031(a). In such a case, the taxpayer's transfer of relinquished property and subsequent receipt of like-kind replacement property is treated as an exchange, and the determination of whether the taxpayer is in actual or constructive receipt of money or other property before the taxpayer actually receives like-kind replacement property is made as if the qualified intermediary is not the agent of the taxpayer.

(ii) Paragraph (g)(4)(i) of this section applies only if the agreement between the taxpayer and the qualified intermediary expressly limits the taxpayer's rights to receive, pledge, borrow, or otherwise obtain the benefits of money or other property held by the qualified intermediary as provided in paragraph (g)(6) of this section.

(iii) A qualified intermediary is a person who -

(A) Is not the taxpayer or a disqualified person (as defined in paragraph (k) of this section), and

(B) Enters into a written agreement with the taxpayer (the "exchange agreement") and, as required by the exchange agreement, acquires the relinquished property from the taxpayer, transfers the relinquished property, acquires the replacement property, and transfers the replacement property to the taxpayer.

(iv) Regardless of whether an intermediary acquires and transfers property under general tax principals, solely for purposes of paragraph (g)(4)(iii)(B) of this section -

(A) An intermediary is treated as acquiring and transferring property if the intermediary acquires and transfers legal title to that property,

(B) An intermediary is treated as acquiring and transferring the relinquished property if the intermediary (either on its own behalf or as the agent of any party to the transaction) enters into an agreement with a person other than the taxpayer for the transfer of the relinquished property to that person and, pursuant to that agreement, the relinquished property is transferred to that person, and

(C) An intermediary is treated as acquiring and transferring replacement property if the intermediary (either on its own behalf or as the agent of any party to the transaction) enters into an agreement with the owner of the replacement property for the transfer of that property and, pursuant to that agreement, the replacement property is transferred to the taxpayer.

(v) Solely for purposes of paragraphs (g)(4)(iii) and (g)(4)(iv) of this section, an intermediary is treated as entering into an agreement if the rights of a party to the agreement are assigned to the intermediary and all parties to that agreement are notified in writing of the assignment on or before the date of the relevent transfer of property. For example, if a taxpayer enters into an agreement for the transfer of relinquished property and thereafter assigns its rights in that agreement to an intermediary and all parties to that agreement are notified in writing of the assignment on or before the date of the transfer of the relinquished property, the intermediary is treated as entering into that agreement. If the relinquished property is transferred pursuant to that agreement, the intermediary is treated as having acquired and transferred the relinquished property.

(vi) Paragraph (g)(4)(i) of this section ceases to apply at the time the taxpayer has an immediate ability or unrestricted right to receive, pledge, borrow, or otherwise obtain the benefits of money or other property held by the qualified intermediary. Rights conferred upon the taxpayer under state law to terminate or dismiss the qualified intermediary are disregarded for this purpose.

(vii) A taxpayer may receive money or other property directly from a party to the transaction other than the qualified intermediary without affecting the application of paragraph (g)(4)(i) of this section.

(5) *Interest and growth factors.* In the case of a deferred exchange, the determination of whether the taxpayer is in actual or constructive receipt of money or other property before the taxpayer actually receives the like-kind replacement property will be made without regard to the fact that the taxpayer is or may be entitled to receive any interest or growth factor with respect to the deferred exchange. The preceding sentence applies only if the agreement pursuant to which the taxpayer is or may be entitled to the interest or growth factor expressly limits the taxpayer's rights to receive the interest or growth factor as provided in paragragh (g)(6) of this section. For additional rules concerning interest or growth factors, see paragraph (h) of this section.

(6) *Additional restrictions on safe harbors under paragraphs (g)(3) through (g)(5).*

(i) An agreement limits a taxpayer's rights as provided in this paragraph (g)(6) only if the agreement provides that the taxpayer has no rights, except as provided in paragraph (g)(6)(ii) and (g)(6)(iii) of this section, to receive, pledge, borrow, or otherwise obtain the benefits of money or other property before the end of the exchange period.

(ii) The agreement may provide that if the taxpayer has not identified replacement property by the end of the identification period, the taxpayer may have rights to receive, pledge, borrow, or othewise obtain the benefits of money or other property at any time after the end of the identification period.

(iii) The agreement may provide that if the taxpayer has identified replacement property, the taxpayer may have rights to receive, pledge, borrow, or otherwise obtain the benefits of money or other property upon or after -

(A) The receipt by the taxpayer of all of the replacement property to which the taxpayer is entitled under the exchange agreement, or

(B) The occurrence after the end of the identification period of a material and substantial contingency that -

(1) Relates to the deferred exchange,

(2) Is provided for in writing, and

(3) Is beyond the control of the taxpayer and of any disqualified person (as defined in paragraph (k) of this section), other than the person obligated to transfer the replacement property to the taxpayer.

(7) *Items disregarded in applying safe harbors under paragraphs (g)(3) through (g)(5).* In determining whether a safe harbor under paragraphs (g)(3) through (g)(5) of this section ceases to apply and whether the taxpayer's rights to receive, pledge, borrow, or otherwise obtain the benefits of money or other property are expressly limited as provided in paragraph (g)(6) of this section, the taxpayer's receipt of or right to receive any of the following items will be disregarded -

(i) Items that a <u>seller</u> may receive as a consequence of the <u>disposition</u> of <u>property</u> and that are not included in the <u>amount</u> realized from the <u>disposition</u> of <u>property</u> (e.g., prorated rents), and

(ii) Transactional items that relate to the <u>disposition</u> of the relinquished <u>property</u> or to the <u>acquisition</u> of the replacement <u>property</u> and appear under local standards in the typical closing <u>statements</u> as the responsibility of a buyer or <u>seller</u> (e.g., <u>commissions</u>, prorated taxes, recording or <u>transfer</u> taxes, and title company fees).

(8) *Examples*. This paragraph <u>(g)</u> may be illustrated by the following <u>examples</u>. Unless otherwise provided in an <u>example</u>, the following <u>facts</u> are assumed: B, a calendar <u>year</u> <u>taxpayer</u>, and C agree to enter into a deferred <u>exchange</u>. Pursuant to their <u>agreement</u>, B is to <u>transfer</u> <u>real property</u> X to C on May 17, 1991. <u>Real property</u> X, which has been held by B for <u>investment</u>, is unencumbered and has a <u>fair market value</u> on May 17, 1991, of $100,000. On or before July 1, 1991 (the end of the <u>identification</u> period), B is to identify replacement <u>property</u> that is of a like kind to <u>real property</u> X. On or before November 13, 1991 (the end of the <u>exchange</u> period), C is required to <u>purchase</u> the <u>property</u> identified by B and to <u>transfer</u> that <u>property</u> to B. To the extent the <u>fair market value</u> of the replacement <u>property</u> <u>transferred</u> to B is greater or less than the <u>fair market value</u> <u>property</u> X, either B or C, as applicable, will make up the difference by paying <u>cash</u> to the other party after the date the replacement <u>property</u> is received by B. The replacement <u>property</u> is identified as provided in <u>paragraph (c)</u> of this section (relating to <u>identification</u> of replacement property) and is of a like kind to <u>real property</u> X (determined without regard to section 1031(a)(3) and this section). B intends to hold any replacement <u>property</u> received for <u>investment</u>.

EXAMPLE 1.

(i) On May 17, 1991, B transfers real property X to C. On the same day, C pays $10,000 to B and deposits $90,000 in escrow as security for C's obligation to perform under the agreement. The escrow agreement provides that B has no rights to receive, pledge, borrow, or otherwise obtain the benefits of the money in escrow before November 14, 1991, except that:

(A) if B fails to identify replacement <u>property</u> on or before July 1, 1991, B may demand the funds in escrow at any time after July 1, 1991; and

(B) if B identifies and receives replacement <u>property</u>, then B may demand the balance of the remaining funds in escrow at any time after B has received the replacement <u>property</u>.

The funds in escrow may be used to purchase the replacement property. The escrow holder is not a disqualified person as defined in paragraph (k) of this section. Pursuant to the terms of the agreement, B identifies replacement property, and C purchases the replacement property using the funds in escrow and tranfers the replacement property to B.

(ii) C's obligation to transfer the replacement property to B was secured by cash held in a qualified escrow account because the escrow holder was not a disqualified person and the escrow agreement expressly limited B's rights to receive, pledge, borrow, or otherwise obtain the benefits of the money in escrow as provided in paragraph (g)(6) of this section. In addition, B did not have the immediate ability or unrestricted right to receive money or other property in escrow before B actually received the like-kind replacement property. Therefore, for purposes of section 1031 and this section, B is determined not to be in actual or constructive receipt of the $90,000 held in escrow before B received the like-kind replacement property. The transfer of real property X by B and B's acquisition of the replacement property qualify as an exchange under section 1031. See paragraph (j) of this section for determining the amount of gain or loss recognized.

EXAMPLE 2.

(i) On May 17, 1991, B transfers real property X to C, and C deposits $100,000 in escrow as security for C's obligation to perform under the agreement. Also on May 17, B identifies real property J as replacement property. The escrow agreement provides that no funds may be paid out without prior written approval of both B and C. The escrow agreement also provides that B has no rights to receive, pledge, borrow, or otherwise obtain the benefits of the money in escrow before November 14, 1991, except that:

(A) B may demand the funds in escrow at any time after the later of July 1, 1991, and the occurrence of any of the following events -

(1) real property J is destroyed, seized, requisitioned, or condemned, or

(2) a determination is made that the regulatory approval necessary for the transfer of real property J cannot be obtained in time for real property J to be transferred to B before the end of the exchange period;

(B) B may demand the funds in escrow at any time after August 14, 1991, if real property J has not been rezoned from residential to commercial use by that date; and

(C) B may demand the funds in escrow at the time B receives <u>real property</u> J or any time thereafter.

Otherwise, B is entitled to all funds in escrow after November 13, 1991. The funds in escrow may be used to <u>purchase</u> the replacement <u>property</u>. The escrow <u>holder</u> is not a disqualified <u>person</u> as described in <u>paragraph (k)</u> of this section. <u>Real property</u> J is not rezoned from residential to commercial use on or before August 14, 1991.

(ii) C's <u>obligation</u> to <u>transfer</u> the replacement <u>property</u> to B was secured by <u>cash</u> held in a qualified escrow <u>account</u> because the escrow <u>holder</u> was not a disqualified <u>person</u> and the escrow <u>agreement</u> expressly limited B's rights to receive, pledge, borrow, or otherwise obtain the <u>benefits</u> of the money in escrow as provided in <u>paragraph (g)(6)</u> of this section. From May 17, 1991, until August 15, 1991, B did not have the immediate ability or unrestricted right to receive money or <u>other property</u> before B actually received the like-kind replacement <u>property</u>. Therefore, for <u>purposes</u> of section 1031 and this section, B is determined not to be in actual or constructive <u>receipt</u> of the $100,000 in escrow from May 17, 1991, until August 15, 1991. However, on August 15, 1991, B had the unrestricted right, upon <u>notice</u>, to draw upon the $100,000 held in escrow. Thus, the <u>safe harbor</u> ceased to apply and B was in constructive <u>receipt</u> of the funds held in escrow. Because B constructively received the full <u>amount</u> of the consideration ($100,000) before B actually received the like-kind replacement <u>property</u>, the transaction is treated as a sale and not as a deferred <u>exchange</u>. The <u>result</u> does not change even if B chose not to demand the funds in escrow and continued to attempt to have <u>real property</u> J rezoned and to receive the <u>property</u> on or before November 13, 1991.

(iii) If <u>real property</u> J had been rezoned on or before August 14, 1991, and C had purchased <u>real property</u> J and <u>transferred</u> it to B on or before November 13, 1991, the transaction would have qualified for nonrecognition of <u>gain or loss</u> under section 1031(a).

EXAMPLE 3.

(i) On May 1, 1991, D offers to purchase real property X for $100,000. However, D is unwilling to participate in a like-kind exchange. B thus enters into an exchange agreement with C whereby B retains C to facilitate an exchange with respect to real property X. C is not a disqualified person as described in <u>paragraph (k)</u> of this section. The exchange agreement between B and C provides that B is to execute and deliver a deed conveying real property X to C who, in turn, is to execute and deliver a deed conveying real property X to D. The exchange agreement expressly limits B's rights to receive, pledge, borrow, or otherwise obtain the benefits of money or other property held by C as provided in paragraph (g)(6) of this section. On May 3, 1991, C enters into an agreement with D to transfer real property X to D for $100,000. On May 17, 1991, B executes and delivers to C a deed conveying real property X to C. On the same date, C executes and delivers to D a deed conveying real property X to D, and D deposits $100,000 in escrow. The escrow holder is not a disqualified person as defined in paragraph (k) of this section and the escrow agreement expressly limits B's rights to receive, pledge, borrow, or otherwise obtain the benefits of money or other property in escrow as provided in paragraph (g)(6) of this section. However, the escrow agreement provides that the money in escrow may be used to purchase replacement property. On June 3, 1991, B identifies real property K as replacement property. On August 9, 1991, E executes and delivers to C a deed conveying real property K to C and $80,000 is released from the escrow and paid to E. On the same date, C executes and delivers to B a deed conveying real property K to B, and the escrow holder pays B $20,000, the balance of the $100,000 sale price of real property X remaining after the purchase of real property K for $80,000.

(ii) B and C entered into an exchange agreement that satisfied the requirements of paragraph (g)(4)(iii)(B) of this section. Regardless of whether C may have acquired and transferred real property X under general tax principles, C is treated as having acquired and transferred real property X because C acquired and transferred legal title to real property X. Similarly, C is treated as having acquired and transferred real property K because C acquired and transferred legal title to real property K. Thus, C was a qualified intermediary. This result is reached for purposes of this section regardless of whether C was B's agent under state law.

(iii) Because the escrow holder was not a disqualified person and the escrow agreement expressly limited B's rights to receive, pledge, borrow, or otherwise obtain the benefits of money or other property in escrow as provided in paragraph (g)(6) of this section, the escrow account was a qualified escrow account. For purposes of section 1031 and this section, therefore, B is determined not to be in actual or constructive receipt of the funds in escrow before B received real property K.

(iv) The exchange agreement between B and C expressly limited B's rights to receive, pledge, borrow, or otherwise obtain the benefits of any money held by C as provided in paragraph (g)(6) of this section. Because C was a qualified intermediary, for purposes of section 1031 and this section B is determined not to be in actual or constructive receipt of any funds held by C before B received real property K. In addition, B's transfer of real property X and acquisition of real property K qualify as an exchange under section 1031. See paragraph (j) of this section for determining the amount of gain or loss recognized.

(v) If the escrow agreement had expressly limited C's rights to receive, pledge, borrow, or otherwise obtain the benefits of money or other property in escrow as provided in paragraph (g)(6) of this section, but had not expressly limited B's rights to receive, pledge, borrow, or otherwise obtain the benefits of that money or other property, the escrow account would not have been a qualified escrow account. Consequently, paragraph (g)(3)(i) of this section would not have been applicable in determining whether B was in actual or constructive receipt of that money or other property before B received real property K.

EXAMPLE 4.

(i) On May 1, 1991, B enters into an agreement to sell real property X to D for $100,000 on May 17, 1991. However, D is unwilling to participate in a like-kind exchange. B thus enters into an exchange agreement with C whereby B retains C to facilitate an exchange with respect to real property X. C is not a disqualified person as described in paragraph (k) of this section. In the exchange agreement between B and C, B assigns to C all of B's rights in the agreement with D. The exchange agreement expressly limits B's rights to receive, pledge, borrow, or otherwise obtain the benefits of money or other property held by C as provided in paragraph (g)(6) of this section. On May 17, 1991, B notifies D in writing of the assignment. On the same date, B executes and delivers to D a deed conveying real property X to D. D pays $10,000 to B and $90,000 to C. On June 1, 1991, B identifies real property L as replacement property. On July 5, 1991, B enters into an agreement to purchase real property L from E for $90,000, assigns its rights in that agreement to C, and notifies E in writing of the assignment. On August 9, 1991, C pays $90,000 to E, and E executes and delivers to B a deed conveying real property L to B.

(ii) The exchange agreement entered into by B and C satisfied the requirements of paragraph (g)(4)(iii)(B) of this section. Because B's rights in its agreements with D and E were assigned to C, and D and E were notified in writing of the assignment on or before the transfer of real properties X and L, respectively, C is treated as entering into those agreements. Because C is treated as entering into an agreement with D for the transfer of real property X and, pursuant to that agreement, real property X was transferred to D, C is treated as acquiring and transferring real property X. Similarly, because C is treated as entering into an agreement with E for the transfer of real property K and, pursuant to that agreement, real property K was transferred to B, C is treated as acquiring and transferring real property K. This result is reached for purposes of this section regardless of whether C was B's agent under state law and regardless of whether C is considered, under general tax principles, to have <u>acquired</u> title or <u>beneficial ownership</u> of the properties. Thus, C was a qualified <u>intermediary</u>.

(iii) The <u>exchange</u> <u>agreement</u> between B and C expressly limited B's rights to receive, pledge, borrow, or otherwise obtain the <u>benefits</u> of the money held by C as provided in <u>paragraph (g)(6)</u> of this section. Thus, B did not have the immediate ability or unrestricted right to receive money or <u>other property</u> held by C before B received <u>real property</u> L. For <u>purposes</u> of section 1031 and this section, therefore, B is determined not to be in actual or constructive <u>receipt</u> of the $90,000 held by C before B received <u>real property</u> L. In addition, the <u>transfer</u> of <u>real property</u> X by B and B's <u>acquisition</u> of <u>real property</u> L qualify as an <u>exchange</u> under section 1031. See <u>paragraph (j)</u> of this section for determining the <u>amount</u> of <u>gain or loss</u> recognized.

EXAMPLE 5.

(i) On May 1, 1991, B enters into an agreement to sell real property X to D for $100,000. However, D is unwilling to participate in a like-kind exchange. B thus enters into an agreement with C whereby B retains C to facilitate an exchange with respect to real property X. C is not a disqualified person as described in <u>paragraph (k)</u> of this section. The agreement between B and C expressly limits B's rights to receive, pledge, borrow, or otherwise obtain the benefits of money or other property held by C as provided in <u>paragraph (g)(6)</u> of this section. C neither enters into an agreement with D to transfer real property X to D nor is assigned B's rights in B's agreement to sell real property X to D. On May 17, 1991, B transfers real property X to D and instructs D to transfer the $100,000 to C. On June 1, 1991, B identifies real property M as replacement property. On August 9, 1991, C purchases real property L from E for $100,000, and E executes and delivers to C a deed conveying real property M to C. On the same date, C executes and delivers to B a deed conveying real property M to B.

(ii) Because B transferred <u>real property</u> X directly to D under B's <u>agreement</u> with D, C did not acquire <u>real property</u> X from B and <u>transfer</u> <u>real property</u> X to D. Moreover, because C did not acquire legal title to <u>real property</u> X, did not enter into an <u>agreement</u> with D to <u>transfer</u> <u>real property</u> X to D, and was not assigned B's rights in B's <u>agreement</u> to sell <u>real property</u> X to D, C is not treated as <u>acquiring</u> and transferring <u>real property</u> X. Thus, C was not a qualified <u>intermediary</u> and paragraph (g)(4))(i) of this section does not apply.

(iii) B did not <u>exchange</u> <u>real property</u> X for <u>real property</u> M. Rather, B sold <u>real property</u> X to D and purchased, through C, <u>real property</u> M. Therefore,

121

the transfer of real property X does not qualify for nonrecognition of gain or loss under section 1031.

(h) *Interest and growth factors -*

(1) *In general.* For purposes of this section, the taxpayer is treated as being entitled to receive interest or a growth factor with respect to a deferred exchange if the amount of money or property the taxpayer is entitled to receive depends upon the length of time elapsed between transfer of the relinquished property and receipt of the replacement property.

(2) *Treatment as interest.* If, as part of a deferred exchange, the taxpayer receives interest or a growth factor, the interest or growth factor will be treated as interest, regardless of whether it is paid to the taxpayer in cash or in property (including property of a like kind). The taxpayer must include the interest or growth factor in income according to the taxpayer's method of accounting. For rules under section 468B(g) relating to the current taxation of qualified escrow accounts, qualified trusts, and other escrow accounts, trusts, and funds used during deferred exchanges of like-kind property, see § 1.468B-6.

(i) [Reserved]

(j) *Determination of gain or loss recognized and the basis of property received in a deferred exchange -*

(1) *In general.* Except as otherwise provided, the amount of gain or loss recognized and the basis of property received in a deferred exchange is determined by applying the rules of section 1031 and the regulations thereunder. See §§ 1.1031(b)-1, 1.1031(c)-1, 1.1031(d)-1, 1.1031(d)-1T, 1.1031(d)-2, and 1.1031(j)-1.

(2) *Coordination with section 453 -*

(i) *Qualified escrow accounts and qualified trusts.* Subject to the limitations of paragraphs (j)(2) (iv) and (v) of this section, in the case of a taxpayer's transfer of relinquished property in which the obligation of the taxpayer's transferee to transfer replacement property to the taxpayer is or may be secured by cash or a cash equivalent, the determination of whether the taxpayer has received a payment for purposes of section 453 and § 15a.453-1(b)(3)(i) of this chapter will be made without regard to the fact that the obligation is or may be so secured if the cash or cash equivalent is held in a qualified escrow account or a qualified trust. This paragraph (j)(2)(i) ceases to apply at the earlier of -

(A) The time described in paragraph (g)(3)(iv) of this section; or

(B) The end of the exchange period.

(ii) *Qualified intermediaries.* Subject to the limitations of paragraphs (j) (2) (iv) and (v) of this section, in the case of a taxpayer's transfer of relinquished property involving a qualified intermediary, the determination of whether the taxpayer has received a payment for purposes of section 453 and § 15a.453-1(b)(3)(i) of this chapter is made as if the qualified intermediary is not the agent of the taxpayer. For purposes of this paragraph (j)(2)(ii), a person who otherwise satisfies the definition of a qualified intermediary is treated as a qualified intermediary even though that person ultimately fails to acquire identified replacement property and transfer it to the taxpayer. This paragraph (j)(2)(ii) ceases to apply at the earlier of -

(A) The time described in paragraph (g)(4)(vi) of this section; or

(B) The end of the exchange period.

(iii) *Transferee indebtedness.* In the case of a transaction described in paragraph (j)(2)(ii) of this section, the receipt by the taxpayer of an evidence of indebtedness of the transferee of the qualified intermediary is treated as the receipt of an evidence of indebtedness of the person acquiring property from the taxpayer for purposes of section 453 and § 15a.453-1(b)(3)(i) of this chapter.

(iv) *Bona fide intent requirement.* The provisions of paragraphs (j)(2) (i) and (ii) of this section do not apply unless the taxpayer has a bona fide intent to enter into a deferred exchange at the beginning of the exchange period. A taxpayer will be treated as having a bona fide intent only if it is reasonable to believe, based on all the facts and circumstances as of the beginning of the exchange period, that like-kind replacement property will be acquired before the end of the exchange period.

(v) *Disqualified property.* The provisions of paragraphs (j)(2) (i) and (ii) of this section do not apply if the relinquished property is disqualified property. For purposes of this paragraph (j)(2), *disqualified property* means property that is not held for productive use in a trade or business or for investment or is property described in section 1031(a)(2).

(vi) *Examples.* This paragraph (j)(2) may be illustrated by the following examples. Unless otherwise provided in an example, the following facts are assumed: B is a calendar year taxpayer who agrees to enter into a deferred exchange. Pursuant to the agreement, B is to transfer real property X. Real property X, which has been held by B for investment, is unencumbered and has a fair market value of $100,000 at the time of transfer. B's adjusted basis in real property X at that time is $60,000. B identifies a single like-kind replacement property before the end of the identification period, and B receives the replacement property before the end of the exchange period. The transaction qualifies as a like-kind exchange under section 1031.

EXAMPLE 1.

(i) On September 22, 1994, B transfers real property X to C and C agrees to acquire like-kind property and deliver it to B. On that date B has a bona fide intent to enter into a deferred exchange. C's obligation, which is not payable on demand or readily tradable, is secured by $100,000 in cash. The $100,000 is deposited by C in an escrow account that is a qualified escrow account under paragraph (g)(3) of this section. The escrow agreement provides that B has no rights to receive, pledge, borrow, or otherwise obtain the benefits of the cash deposited in the escrow account until the earlier of the date the replacement property is delivered to B or the end of the exchange period. On March 11, 1995, C acquires replacement property having a fair market value of $80,000 and delivers the replacement property to B. The $20,000 in cash remaining in the qualified escrow account is distributed to B at that time.

(ii) Under section 1031(b), B recognizes gain to the extent of the $20,000 in cash that B receives in the exchange. Under paragraph (j)(2)(i) of this section, the qualified escrow account is disregarded for purposes of section 453 and § 15a.453-1(b)(3)(i) of this chapter in determining whether B is in receipt of payment. Accordingly, B's receipt of C's obligation on September 22, 1994, does not constitute a payment. Instead, B is treated as receiving payment on March 11, 1995, on receipt of the $20,000 in cash from the qualified escrow account. Subject to the other requirements of sections 453 and 453A, B may report the $20,000 gain in 1995 under the installment method. See section 453(f)(6) for special rules for determining total contract price and gross profit in the case of an exchange described in section 1031(b).

EXAMPLE 2.

(i) D offers to purchase real property X but is unwilling to participate in a like-kind exchange. B thus enters into an exchange agreement with C whereby B retains C to facilitate an exchange with respect to real property X. On September 22, 1994, pursuant to the agreement, B transfers real property X to C who transfers it to D for $100,000 in cash. On that date B has a bona fide intent to enter into a deferred exchange. C is a qualified intermediary under paragraph (g)(4) of this section. The exchange agreement provides that B has no rights to receive, pledge, borrow, or otherwise obtain the benefits of the money held by C until the earlier of the date the replacement property is delivered to B or the end of the exchange period. On March 11, 1995, C acquires replacement property having a fair market value of $80,000 and delivers it, along with the remaining $20,000 from the transfer of real property X to B.

(ii) Under section 1031(b), B recognizes gain to the extent of the $20,000 cash B receives in the exchange. Under paragraph (j)(2)(ii) of this section, any agency relationship between B and C is disregarded for purposes of section 453 and § 15a.453-1(b)(3)(i) of this chapter in determining whether B is in receipt of payment. Accordingly, B is not treated as having received payment on September 22, 1994, on C's receipt of payment from D for the relinquished property. Instead, B is treated as receiving payment on March 11, 1995, on receipt of the $20,000 in cash from C. Subject to the other requirements of sections 453 and 453A, B may report the $20,000 gain in 1995 under the installment method.

EXAMPLE 3.

(i) D offers to purchase real property X but is unwilling to participate in a like-kind exchange. B enters into an exchange agreement with C whereby B retains C as a qualified intermediary to facilitate an exchange with respect to real property X. On December 1, 1994, pursuant to the agreement, B transfers real property X to C who transfers it to D for $100,000 in cash. On that date B has a bona fide intent to enter into a deferred exchange. The exchange agreement provides that B has no rights to receive, pledge, borrow, or otherwise obtain the benefits of the cash held by C until the earliest of the end of the identification period if B has not identified replacement property, the date the replacement property is delivered to B, or the end of the exchange period. Although B has a bona fide intent to enter into a deferred exchange at the beginning of the exchange period, B does not identify or acquire any replacement property. In 1995, at the end of the identification period, C delivers the entire $100,000 from the sale of real property X to B.

(ii) Under section 1001, B realizes gain to the extent of the amount realized ($100,000) over the adjusted basis in real property X ($60,000), or $40,000. Because B has a bona fide intent at the beginning of the exchange period to enter into a deferred exchange, paragraph (j)(2)(iv) of this section does not make paragraph (j)(2)(ii) of this section inapplicable even though B fails to acquire replacement property. Further, under paragraph (j)(2)(ii) of this section, C is a qualified intermediary even though C does not acquire and transfer replacement property to B. Thus, any agency relationship between B and C is disregarded for purposes of section 453 and § 15a.453-1(b)(3)(i) of this chapter in determining whether B is in receipt of payment. Accordingly, B is not treated as having received payment on December 1, 1994, on C's receipt of payment from D for the relinquished property. Instead, B is treated as receiving payment at the end of the identification period in 1995 on receipt

125

of the $100,000 in <u>cash</u> from C. Subject to the <u>other requirements</u> of sections 453 and 453A, B may report the $40,000 gain in 1995 under the <u>installment method</u>.

EXAMPLE 4.

(i) D offers to purchase real property X but is unwilling to participate in a like-kind exchange. B thus enters into an exchange agreement with C whereby B retains C to facilitate an exchange with respect to real property X. C is a qualified intermediary under <u>paragraph (g)(4)</u> of this section. On September 22, 1994, pursuant to the agreement, B transfers real property X to C who then transfers it to D for $80,000 in cash and D's 10-year installment obligation for $20,000. On that date B has a bona fide intent to enter into a deferred exchange. The exchange agreement provides that B has no rights to receive, pledge, borrow, or otherwise obtain the benefits of the money or other property held by C until the earlier of the date the replacement property is delivered to B or the end of the exchange period. D's obligation bears adequate stated interest and is not payable on demand or readily tradable. On March 11, 1995, C acquires replacement property having a fair market value of $80,000 and delivers it, along with the $20,000 installment obligation, to B.

(ii) Under section 1031(b), $20,000 of B's gain (i.e., the <u>amount</u> of the <u>installment obligation</u> B receives in the exchange) does not qualify for nonrecognition under section 1031(a). Under paragraphs (j)(2) <u>(ii)</u> and <u>(iii)</u> of this section, B's <u>receipt</u> of D's <u>obligation</u> is treated as the <u>receipt</u> of an <u>obligation</u> of the <u>person</u> <u>acquiring</u> the <u>property</u> for <u>purposes</u> of section 453 and § 15a.453-1(b)(3)(i) <u>of this chapter</u> in determining whether B is in <u>receipt</u> of <u>payment</u>. Accordingly, B's <u>receipt</u> of the <u>obligation</u> is not treated as a <u>payment</u>. Subject to the <u>other requirements</u> of sections 453 and 453A, B may report the $20,000 gain under the <u>installment method</u> on receiving <u>payments</u> from D on the <u>obligation</u>.

EXAMPLE 5.

(i) B is a corporation that has held real property X to expand its manufacturing operations. However, at a meeting in November 1994, B's directors decide that real property X is not suitable for the planned expansion, and authorize a like-kind exchange of this property for property that would be suitable for the planned expansion. B enters into an exchange agreement with C whereby B retains C as a qualified intermediary to facilitate an exchange with respect to real property X. On November 28, 1994, pursuant to the agreement, B transfers real property X to C, who then transfers it to D for $100,000 in cash. The exchange agreement does not include any limitations or conditions that make it unreasonable to believe that like-kind replacement property will be acquired before the end of the exchange period. The exchange agreement provides that B has no rights to receive, pledge, borrow, or otherwise obtain the benefits of the cash held by C until the earliest of the end of the identification period, if B has not identified replacement property, the date the replacement property is delivered to B, or the end of the exchange period. In early January 1995, B's directors meet and decide that it is not feasible to proceed with the planned expansion due to a business downturn reflected in B's preliminary financial reports for the last quarter of 1994. Thus, B's directors instruct C to stop seeking replacement property. C delivers the $100,000 cash to B on January 12, 1995, at the end of the identification period. Both the decision to exchange real property X for other property and the decision to cease seeking replacement property because of B's business downturn are recorded in the minutes of the directors' meetings. There are no other facts or circumstances that would indicate whether, on November 28, 1994, B had a bona fide intent to enter into a deferred like-kind exchange.

(ii) Under section 1001, B realizes gain to the extent of the amount realized ($100,000) over the adjusted basis of real property X ($60,000), or $40,000. The directors' authorization of a like-kind exchange, the terms of the exchange agreement with C, and the absence of other relevant facts, indicate that B had a bona fide intent at the beginning of the exchange period to enter into a deferred like-kind exchange. Thus, paragraph (j)(2)(iv) of this section does not make paragraph (j)(2)(ii) of this section inapplicable, even though B fails to acquire replacement property. Further, under paragraph (j)(2)(ii) of this section, C is a qualified intermediary, even though C does not transfer replacement property to B. Thus, any agency relationship between B and C is disregarded for purposes of section 453 and § 15a.453-1(b)(3)(i) of this chapter in determining whether B is in receipt of payment. Accordingly, B is not treated as having received payment until January 12, 1995, on receipt of the $100,000 cash from C. Subject to the other requirements of sections 453 and 453A, B may report the $40,000 gain in 1995 under the installment method.

EXAMPLE 6.

(i) B has held real property X for use in its trade or business, but decides to transfer that property because it is no longer suitable for B's planned expansion of its commercial enterprise. B and D agree to enter into a deferred exchange. Pursuant to their agreement, B transfers real property X to D on September 22, 1994, and D deposits $100,000 cash in a qualified escrow account as security for D's obligation under the agreement to transfer replacement property to B before the end of the exchange period. D's obligation is not payable on demand or readily tradable. The agreement provides that B is not required to accept any property that is not zoned for commercial use. Before the end of the identification period, B identifies real properties J, K, and L, all zoned for residential use, as replacement properties. Any one of these properties, rezoned for commercial use, would be suitable for B's planned expansion. In recent years, the zoning board with jurisdiction over properties J, K, and L has rezoned similar properties for commercial use. The escrow agreement provides that B has no rights to receive, pledge, borrow, or otherwise obtain the benefits of the money in the escrow account until the earlier of the time that the zoning board determines, after the end of the identification period, that it will not rezone the properties for commercial use or the end of the exchange period. On January 5, 1995, the zoning board decides that none of the properties will be rezoned for commercial use. Pursuant to the exchange agreement, B receives the $100,000 cash from the escrow on January 5, 1995. There are no other facts or circumstances that would indicate whether, on September 22, 1994, B had a bona fide intent to enter into a deferred like-kind exchange.

(ii) Under section 1001, B realizes gain to the extent of the <u>amount</u> realized ($100,000) over the <u>adjusted basis</u> of <u>real property</u> X ($60,000), or $40,000. The <u>terms</u> of the <u>exchange</u> <u>agreement</u> with D, the <u>identification</u> of properties J, K, and L, the efforts to have those properties rezoned for commercial <u>purposes</u>, and the absence of other relevant <u>facts</u>, indicate that B had a bona fide intent at the beginning of the <u>exchange</u> period to enter into a deferred <u>exchange</u>. Moreover, the <u>limitations</u> imposed in the <u>exchange</u> <u>agreement</u> on acceptable replacement <u>property</u> do not make it unreasonable to believe that like-kind replacement <u>property</u> would be <u>acquired</u> before the end of the <u>exchange</u> period. Therefore, <u>paragraph (j)(2)(iv)</u> of this section does not make <u>paragraph (j)(2)(i)</u> of this section inapplicable even though B fails to acquire replacement <u>property</u>. Thus, for <u>purposes</u> of section 453 and § 15a.453-1(b)(3) (i) <u>of this chapter</u>, the qualified escrow <u>account</u> is disregarded in determining whether B is in <u>receipt</u> of <u>payment</u>. Accordingly, B is not treated as having received <u>payment</u> on September 22, 1994, on D's deposit of the $100,000 <u>cash</u> into the qualified escrow <u>account</u>. Instead, B is treated as receiving <u>payment</u> on January 5, 1995. Subject to the <u>other requirements</u> of sections 453 and 453A, B may report the $40,000 gain in 1995 under the <u>installment method</u>.

(vii) *Effective date.* This paragraph (j)(2) is effective for <u>transfers</u> of <u>property</u> occurring on or after April 20, 1994. <u>Taxpayers</u> may apply this paragraph (j)(2) to <u>transfers</u> of <u>property</u> occurring before April 20, 1994, but on or after June 10, 1991, if those <u>transfers</u> otherwise meet the <u>requirements</u> of § 1.1031(k)-1. In addition, <u>taxpayers</u> may apply this paragraph (j)(2) to <u>transfers</u> of <u>property</u> occurring before June 10, 1991, but on or after May 16, 1990, if those <u>transfers</u> otherwise meet the <u>requirements</u> of § 1.1031(k)-1 or follow the guidance of IA-237-84 published in 1990-1, C.B. See § 601.601(d)(2)(ii)(*b*) of this chapter.

(3) *Examples.* This paragraph (j) may be illustrated by the following examples. Unless otherwise provided in an example, the following facts are assumed: B, a calendar year taxpayer, and C agree to enter into a deferred exchange. Pursuant to their agreement, B is to transfer real property X to C on May 17, 1991. Real property X, which has been held by B for investment, is unencumbered and has a fair market value on May 17, 1991, of $100,000. B's adjusted basis in real property X is $40,000. On or before July 1, 1991 (the end of the identification period), B is to identify replacement property that is of a like kind to real property X. On or before November 13, 1991 (the end of the exchange period), C is required to purchase the property identified by B and to transfer that property to B. To the extent the fair market value of the replacement property transferred to B is greater or less than the fair market value of real property X, either B or C, as applicable, will make up the difference by paying cash to the other party after the date the replacement property is received. The replacement property is identified as provided in paragraph (c) of this section and is of a like kind to real property X (determined without regard to section 1031(a)(3) and this section). B intends to hold any replacement property received for investment.

EXAMPLE 1.

(i) On May 17, 1991, B transfers real property X to C and identifies real property R as replacement property. On June 3, 1991, C transfers $10,000 to B. On September 4, 1991, C purchases real property R for $90,000 and transfers real property R to B.

(ii) The $10,000 received by B is "money or other property" for purposes of section 1031 and the regulations thereunder. Under section 1031(b), B recognizes gain in the amount of $10,000. Under section 1031(d), B's basis in real property R is $40,000 (i.e., B's basis in real property X ($40,000), decreased in the amount of money received ($10,000), and increased in the amount of gain recognized ($10,000) in the deferred exchange).

EXAMPLE 2.

(i) On May 17, 1991, B transfers real property X to C and identifies real property S as replacement property, and C transfers $10,000 to B. On September 4, 1991, C purchases real property S for $100,000 and transfers real property S to B. On the same day, B transfers $10,000 to C.

(ii) The $10,000 received by B is "money or other property" for purposes of section 1031 and the regulations thereunder. Under section 1031(b), B recognizes gain in the amount of $10,000. Under section 1031(d), B's basis in real property S is $50,000 (i.e., B's basis in real property X ($40,000), decreased in the amount of money received ($10,000), increased in the amount of gain recognized ($10,000), and increased in the amount of the additional consideration paid by B ($10,000) in the deferred exchange).

EXAMPLE 3.

(i) Under the exchange agreement, B has the right at all times to demand $100,000 in cash in lieu of replacement property. On May 17, 1991, B transfers real property X to C and identifies real property T as replacement property. On September 4, 1991, C purchases real property T for $100,000 and transfers real property T to B.

(ii) Because B has the right on May 17, 1991, to demand $100,000 in cash in lieu of replacement property, B is in constructive receipt of the $100,000 on that date. Thus, the transaction is a sale and not an exchange, and the $60,000 gain realized by B in the transaction (i.e., $100,000 amount realized less $40,000 adjusted basis) is recognized. Under section 1031(d), B's basis in real property T is $100,000.

EXAMPLE 4.

(i) Under the exchange agreement, B has the right at all times to demand up to $30,000 in cash and the balance in replacement propertry instead of receiving replacement property in the amount of $100,000. On May 17, 1991, B transfers real property X to C and identifies real property U as replacement property. On September 4, 1991, C purchases real property U for $100,000 and transfers real property U to B.

(ii) The transaction qualifies as a deferred exchange under section 1031 and this section. However, because B had the right on May 17, 1991, to demand up to $30,000 in cash, B is in constructive receipt of $30,000 on that date. Under section 1031(b), B recognizes gain in the amount of $30,000. Under section 1031(d), B's basis in real property U is $70,000 (i.e., B's basis in real property X ($40,000), decreased in the amount of money that B received ($30,000), increased in the amount of gain recognized ($30,000), and increased in the amount of additional consideration paid by B ($30,000) in the deferred exchange).

EXAMPLE 5.

(i) Assume real property X is encumbered by a mortgage of $30,000. On May 17, 1991, B transfers real property X to C and identifies real property V as replacement property, and C assumes the $30,000 mortgage on real property X. Real property V is encumbered by a $20,000 mortgage. On July 5, 1991, C purchases real property V for $90,000 by paying $70,000 and assuming the mortgage and transfers real property V to B with B assuming the mortgage.

(ii) The consideration received by B in the form of the <u>liability</u> assumed by C ($30,000) is offset by the consideration given by B in the form of the <u>liability</u> assumed by B ($20,000). The excess of the <u>liability</u> assumed by C over the <u>liability</u> assumed by B, $10,000, is treated as "money or <u>other property</u>." See § 1.1031(b)-1(c). Thus, B recognizes gain under section 1031(b) in the <u>amount</u> of $10,000. Under section 1031(d), B's basis in <u>real property</u> V is $40,000 (i.e., B's basis in <u>real property</u> X ($40,000), decreased in the <u>amount</u> of money that B is treated as receiving in the form of the <u>liability</u> assumed by C ($30,000), increased in the <u>amount</u> of money that B is treated as paying in the form of the <u>liability</u> assumed by B ($20,000), and increased in the <u>amount</u> of the gain recognized ($10,000) in the deferred exchange).

(k) *Definition of disqualified person.*

(1) For <u>purposes</u> of this section, a disqualified <u>person</u> is a <u>person</u> described in paragraph (k)(2), (k)(3), or (k)(4) of this section.

(2) The <u>person</u> is the agent of the <u>taxpayer</u> at the time of the transaction. For this <u>purpose</u>, a <u>person</u> who has acted as the <u>taxpayer</u>'s <u>employee</u>, attorney, accountant, <u>investment</u> banker or <u>broker</u>, or real estate agent or <u>broker</u> within the 2-year period ending on the date of the <u>transfer</u> of the first of the relinquished properties is treated as an agent of the <u>taxpayer</u> at the time of the transaction. Solely for <u>purposes</u> of this paragraph (k)(2), performance of the following <u>services</u> will not be taken into <u>account</u> -

    (i) <u>Services</u> for the <u>taxpayer</u> with respect to <u>exchanges</u> of <u>property</u> intended to qualify for nonrecognition of <u>gain or loss</u> under section 1031; and

    (ii) Routine financial, title insurance, escrow, or <u>trust</u> <u>services</u> for the <u>taxpayer</u> by a <u>financial institution</u>, title <u>insurance company</u>, or escrow company.

(3) The <u>person</u> and the <u>taxpayer</u> bear a relationship described in either section 267(b) or section 707(b) (determined by substituting in each section "10 percent" for "50 percent" each place it appears).

(4)

    (i) Except as provided in <u>paragraph (k)(4)(ii)</u> of this section, the <u>person</u> and a <u>person</u> described in <u>paragraph (k)(2)</u> of this section bear a relationship described in either section 267(b) or 707(b) (determined by substituting in each section "10 percent" for "50 percent" each place it appears).

(ii) In the case of a <u>transfer</u> of relinquished <u>property</u> made by a <u>taxpayer</u> on or after January 17, 2001, <u>paragraph (k)(4)(i)</u> of this section does not apply to a <u>bank</u> (as <u>defined</u> in section 581) or a <u>bank</u> affiliate if, but for this paragraph (k)(4)(ii), the <u>bank</u> or <u>bank</u> affiliate would be a disqualified <u>person</u> under <u>paragraph (k)(4)(i)</u> of this section solely because it is a <u>member</u> of the same <u>controlled group</u> (as determined under section 267(f)(1), substituting "10 percent" for "50 percent' where it appears) as a <u>person</u> that has provided <u>investment</u> banking or brokerage <u>services</u> to the <u>taxpayer</u> within the 2-year period described in <u>paragraph (k)(2)</u> of this section. For <u>purposes</u> of this paragraph (k)(4)(ii), a <u>bank</u> affiliate is a <u>corporation</u> whose principal <u>activity</u> is rendering <u>services</u> to facilitate <u>exchanges</u> of <u>property</u> intended to qualify for nonrecognition of gain under section 1031 and all of whose <u>stock</u> is owned by either a <u>bank</u> or a <u>bank</u> <u>holding company</u> (within the meaning of section 2(a) of the <u>Bank Holding Company Act of 1956</u> (<u>12 U.S.C. 1841(a)</u>).

(5) This paragraph <u>(k)</u> may be illustrated by the following <u>examples</u>. Unless otherwise provided, the following <u>facts</u> are assumed: On May 1, 1991, B enters into an <u>exchange</u> agreement (as <u>defined</u> in <u>paragraph (g)(4)(iii)(B)</u> of this section) with C whereby B retains C to facilitate an <u>exchange</u> with respect to <u>real property</u> X. On May 17, 1991, pursuant to the <u>agreement</u>, B executes and delivers to C a deed conveying <u>real property</u> X to C. C has no relationship to B described in paragraph (k)(2), (k)(3), or (k)(4) of this section.

EXAMPLE 1.

(i) C is B's accountant and has rendered accounting services to B within the 2-year period ending on May 17, 1991, other than with respect to exchanges of property intended to qualify for nonrecognition of gain or loss under section 1031.

(ii) C is a disqualified <u>person</u> because C has acted as B's accountant within the 2-year period ending on May 17, 1991.

(iii) If C had not acted as B's accountant within the 2-year period ending on May 17, 1991, or if C had acted as B's accountant within that period only with respect to <u>exchanges</u> intended to qualify for nonrecognition of <u>gain or loss</u> under section 1031, C would not have been a disqualified <u>person</u>.

Example 2.

    (i) C, which is engaged in the trade or business of acting as an intermediary to facilitate deferred exchanges, is a wholly owned subsidiary of an escrow company that has performed routine escrow services for B in the past. C has previously been retained by B to act as an intermediary in prior section 1031 exchanges.

    (ii) C is not a disqualified person notwithstanding the intermediary services previously provided by C to B (see paragraph (k)(2)(i) of this section) and notwithstanding the combination of C's relationship to the escrow company and the escrow services previously provided by the escrow company to B (see paragraph (k)(2)(ii) of this section).

Example 3.

    (i) C is a corporation that is only engaged in the trade or business of acting as an intermediary to facilitate deferred exchanges. Each of 10 law firms owns 10 percent of the outstanding stock of C. One of the 10 law firms that owns 10 percent of C is M. J is the managing partner of M and is the president of C. J, in his capacity as a partner in M, has also rendered legal advice to B within the 2-year period ending on May 17, 1991, on matters other than exchanges intended to qualify for nonrecognition of gain or loss under section 1031.

    (ii) J and M are disqualified persons. C, however, is not a disqualified person because neither J nor M own, directly or indirectly, more than 10 percent of the stock of C. Similarly, J's participation in the management of C does not make C a disqualified person.

(l) [Reserved]

(m) *Definition of fair market value.* For purposes of this section, the fair market value of property means the fair market value of the property without regard to any liabilities secured by the property.

(n) *No inference with respect to actual or constructive receipt rules outside of section 1031.* The rules provided in this section relating to actual or constructive receipt are intended to be rules for determining whether there is actual or constructive receipt in the case of a deferred exchange. No inference is intended regarding the application of these rules for purposes of determining whether actual or constructive receipt exists for any other purpose.

(o) *Effective date.* This section applies to <u>transfers</u> of <u>property</u> made by a <u>taxpayer</u> on or after June 10, 1991. However, a <u>transfer of property</u> made by a <u>taxpayer</u> on or after May 16, 1990, but before June 10, 1991, will be treated as complying with section 1031 (a) (3) and this section if the deferred <u>exchange</u> satisfies either the provision of this section or the provisions of the <u>notice</u> of proposed rulemaking published in the FEDERAL REGISTER on May 16, 1990 (<u>55 FR 20278</u>).

APPENDIX C

Part III

Administrative, Procedural, and Miscellaneous

26 CFR 1.1031(a)-1: Property held for productive use in trade or business or for investment; 1.1031(k)-1: Treatment of deferred exchanges.

Rev. Proc. 2000-37

SECTION 1. PURPOSE

This revenue procedure provides a safe harbor under which the Internal Revenue Service will not challenge (a) the qualification of property as either "replacement property" or "relinquished property" (as defined in § 1.1031(k)-1(a) of the Income Tax Regulations) for purposes of § 1031 of the Internal Revenue Code and the regulations thereunder or (b) the treatment of the "exchange accommodation titleholder" as the beneficial owner of such property for federal income tax purposes, if the property is held in a "qualified exchange accommodation arrangement" (QEAA), as defined in section 4.02 of this revenue procedure.

SECTION 2. BACKGROUND

.01 Section 1031(a)(1) provides that no gain or loss is recognized on the exchange of property held for productive use in a trade or business or for investment if the property is exchanged solely for property of like kind that is to be held either for productive use in a trade or business or for investment.

.02 Section 1031(a)(3) provides that property received by the taxpayer is not treated as like-kind property if it: (a) is not identified as property to be received in the exchange on or before the day that is 45 days after the date on which the taxpayer transfers the relinquished property; or (b) is received after the earlier of the date that is 180 days after the date on which the taxpayer transfers the relinquished property, or the due date (determined with regard to extension) for the transferor's federal income tax return for the year in which the transfer of the relinquished property occurs.

.03 Determining the owner of property for federal income tax purposes requires an analysis of all of the facts and circumstances. As a general rule, the party that bears the economic burdens and benefits of ownership will be considered the owner of property for federal income tax purposes. See Rev. Rul. 82-144, 1982-2 C.B. 34.

.04 On April 25, 1991, the Treasury Department and the Service promulgated final regulations under § 1.1031(k)-1 providing rules for deferred like-kind exchanges under § 1031(a)(3). The preamble to the final regulations states that the deferred exchange rules under § 1031(a)(3) do not apply to reverse-Starker exchanges (i.e., exchanges where the replacement property is acquired before the relinquished property is transferred) and consequently that the final regulations do not apply to such exchanges. T.D. 8346, 1991-1 C.B. 150, 151; see Starker v. United States, 602 F.2d 1341 (9th Cir. 1979). However, the preamble indicates that Treasury and the Service will continue to study the applicability of the general rule of § 1031(a)(1) to these transactions. T.D. 8346, 1991-1 C.B. 150, 151.

.05 Since the promulgation of the final regulations under § 1.1031(k)-1, taxpayers have engaged in a wide variety of transactions, including so-called "parking" transactions, to facilitate reverse like-kind exchanges. Parking transactions typically are designed to "park" the desired replacement property with an accommodation party until such time as the taxpayer arranges for the transfer of the relinquished property to the ultimate transferee in a simultaneous or deferred exchange. Once such a transfer is arranged, the taxpayer transfers the relinquished property to the accommodation party in exchange for the replacement property, and the accommodation party then transfers the relinquished property to the ultimate transferee. In other situations, an accommodation party may acquire the desired replacement property on behalf of the taxpayer and immediately exchange such property with the taxpayer for the relinquished property, thereafter holding the relinquished property until the taxpayer arranges for a transfer of such property to the ultimate transferee. In the parking arrangements, taxpayers attempt to arrange the transaction so that the accommodation party has enough of the benefits and burdens relating to the property so that the accommodation party will be treated as the owner for federal income tax purposes.

.06 Treasury and the Service have determined that it is in the best interest of sound tax administration to provide taxpayers with a workable means of qualifying their transactions under § 1031 in situations where the taxpayer has a genuine intent to accomplish a like-kind exchange at the time that it arranges for the acquisition of the replacement property and actually accomplishes the exchange within a short time thereafter. Accordingly, this revenue procedure provides a safe harbor that allows a taxpayer to treat the accommodation party as the owner of the property for federal income tax purposes, thereby enabling the taxpayer to accomplish a qualifying like-kind exchange.

SECTION 3. SCOPE

.01 Exclusivity. This revenue procedure provides a safe harbor for the qualification under § 1031 of certain arrangements between taxpayers and exchange accommodation titleholders and provides for the treatment of the exchange accommodation titleholder as the beneficial owner of the property for federal income tax purposes. These provisions apply only in the limited context described in this revenue procedure. The principles set forth in this revenue procedure have no application to any federal income tax determinations other than determinations that involve arrangements qualifying for the safe harbor.

.02 No inference. No inference is intended with respect to the federal income tax treatment of arrangements similar to those described in this revenue procedure that were entered into prior to the effective date of this revenue procedure. Further, the Service recognizes that "parking" transactions can be accomplished outside of the safe harbor provided in this revenue procedure. Accordingly, no inference is intended with respect to the federal income tax treatment of "parking" transactions that do not satisfy the terms of the safe harbor provided in this revenue procedure, whether entered into prior to or after the effective date of this revenue procedure.

.03 Other issues. Services for the taxpayer in connection with a person's role as the exchange accommodation titleholder in a QEAA shall not be taken into account in determining whether that person or a related person is a disqualified person (as defined in § 1.1031(k)-1(k)).

137

Even though property will not fail to be treated as being held in a QEAA as a result of one or more arrangements described in section 4.03 of this revenue procedure, the Service still may recast an amount paid pursuant to such an arrangement as a fee paid to the exchange accommodation titleholder for acting as an exchange accommodation titleholder to the extent necessary to reflect the true economic substance of the arrangement. Other federal income tax issues implicated, but not addressed, in this revenue procedure include the treatment, for federal income tax purposes, of payments described in section 4.03(7) and whether an exchange accommodation titleholder may be precluded from claiming depreciation deductions (e.g., as a dealer) with respect to the relinquished property or the replacement property.

.04 <u>Effect of Noncompliance</u>. If the requirements of this revenue procedure are not satisfied (for example, the property subject to a QEAA is not transferred within the time period provided), then this revenue procedure does not apply. Accordingly, the determination of whether the taxpayer or the exchange accommodation titleholder is the owner of the property for federal income tax purposes, and the proper treatment of any transactions entered into by or between the parties, will be made without regard to the provisions of this revenue procedure.

SECTION 4. QUALIFIED EXCHANGE ACCOMMODATION ARRANGEMENTS

.01 <u>Generally</u>. The Service will not challenge the qualification of property as either "replacement property" or "relinquished property" (as defined in § 1.1031(k)-1(a)) for purposes of § 1031 and the regulations thereunder, or the treatment of the exchange accommodation titleholder as the beneficial owner of such property for federal income tax purposes, if the property is held in a QEAA.

.02 <u>Qualified Exchange Accommodation Arrangements</u>. For purposes of this revenue procedure, property is held in a QEAA if all of the following requirements are met:

Part III

Administrative, Procedural, and Miscellaneous

26 CFR 601.105: Examination of returns and claims for refund, credit, or abatement; determination of correct tax liability.
(Also Part 1, §§ 280A, 1031).

Rev. Proc. 2008-16

SECTION 1. PURPOSE

This revenue procedure provides a safe harbor under which the Internal

Revenue Service (the "Service") will not challenge whether a dwelling unit qualifies as

property held for productive use in a trade or business or for investment for purposes of

§ 1031 of the Internal Revenue Code.

SECTION 2. BACKGROUND

.01 Section 1031(a) provides that no gain or loss is recognized on the exchange

of property held for productive use in a trade or business or for investment (relinquished

property) if the property is exchanged solely for property of like kind that is to be held

either for productive use in a trade or business or for investment (replacement property).

Under § 1.1031(a)-(1)(a)(1) of the Income Tax Regulations, property held for productive use in a trade or business may be exchanged for property held for investment, and property held for investment may be exchanged for property held for productive use in a trade or business.

.02 Rev. Rul. 59-229, 1959-2 C.B. 180, concludes that gain or loss from an exchange of personal residences may not be deferred under § 1031 because the residences are not property held for productive use in a trade or business or for investment.

.03 Section 2.05 of Rev. Proc. 2005-14, 2005-1 C.B. 528, states that § 1031 does not apply to property that is used solely as a personal residence.

.04 In *Moore v. Commissioner*, T.C. Memo. 2007-134, the taxpayers exchanged one lakeside vacation home for another. Neither home was ever rented. Both were used by the taxpayers only for personal purposes. The taxpayers claimed that the exchange of the homes was a like-kind exchange under § 1031 because the properties were expected to appreciate in value and thus were held for investment. The Tax Court held, however, that the properties were held for personal use and that the "mere hope or expectation that property may be sold at a gain cannot establish an investment intent if the taxpayer uses the property as a residence."

.05 In *Starker v. United States*, 602 F.2d 1341, 1350 (9th Cir. 1979), the Ninth Circuit held that a personal residence of a taxpayer was not eligible for exchange under § 1031, explaining that "[it] has long been the rule that use of property solely as a personal residence is antithetical to its being held for investment."

.06 The Service recognizes that many taxpayers hold dwelling units primarily for the production of current rental income, but also use the properties occasionally for personal purposes. In the interest of sound tax administration, this revenue procedure provides taxpayers with a safe harbor under which a dwelling unit will qualify as property held for productive use in a trade or business or for investment under § 1031 even though a taxpayer occasionally uses the dwelling unit for personal purposes.

SECTION 3. SCOPE

.01 In general. This revenue procedure applies to a dwelling unit, as defined in section 3.02 of this revenue procedure, that meets the qualifying use standards in section 4.02 of this revenue procedure.

.02 Dwelling unit. For purposes of this revenue procedure, a dwelling unit is real property improved with a house, apartment, condominium, or similar improvement that provides basic living accommodations including sleeping space, bathroom and cooking facilities.

SECTION 4. APPLICATION

.01 In general. The Service will not challenge whether a dwelling unit as defined in section 3.02 of this revenue procedure qualifies under § 1031 as property held for productive use in a trade or business or for investment if the qualifying use standards in section 4.02 of this revenue procedure are met for the dwelling unit.

.02 Qualifying use standards.

(1) Relinquished property. A dwelling unit that a taxpayer intends to be relinquished property in a § 1031 exchange qualifies as property held for productive use in a trade or business or for investment if:

(a) The dwelling unit is owned by the taxpayer for at least 24 months immediately before the exchange (the "qualifying use period"); and

(b) Within the qualifying use period, in each of the two 12-month periods immediately preceding the exchange,

(i) The taxpayer rents the dwelling unit to another person or persons at a fair rental for 14 days or more, and

(ii) The period of the taxpayer's personal use of the dwelling unit does not exceed the greater of 14 days or 10 percent of the number of days during the 12-month period that the dwelling unit is rented at a fair rental.

For this purpose, the first 12-month period immediately preceding the exchange ends on the day before the exchange takes place (and begins 12 months prior to that day) and the second 12-month period ends on the day before the first 12-month period begins (and begins 12 months prior to that day).

(2) Replacement property. A dwelling unit that a taxpayer intends to be replacement property in a § 1031 exchange qualifies as property held for productive use in a trade or business or for investment if:

(a) The dwelling unit is owned by the taxpayer for at least 24 months immediately after the exchange (the "qualifying use period"); and

(b) Within the qualifying use period, in each of the two 12-month periods immediately after the exchange,

(i) The taxpayer rents the dwelling unit to another person or persons at a fair rental for 14 days or more, and

(ii) The period of the taxpayer's personal use of the dwelling unit does not exceed

the greater of 14 days or 10 percent of the number of days during the 12-month period

that the dwelling unit is rented at a fair rental.

For this purpose, the first 12-month period immediately after the exchange begins on

the day after the exchange takes place and the second 12-month period begins on the

day after the first 12-month period ends.

.03 <u>Personal use</u>. For purposes of this revenue procedure, personal use of a

dwelling unit occurs on any day on which a taxpayer is deemed to have used the

dwelling unit for personal purposes under § 280A(d)(2) (taking into account

§ 280A(d)(3) but not § 280A(d)(4)).

.04 <u>Fair rental</u>. For purposes of this revenue procedure, whether a dwelling unit

is rented at a fair rental is determined based on all of the facts and circumstances that

exist when the rental agreement is entered into. All rights and obligations of the parties

to the rental agreement are taken into account.

.05 <u>Special rule for replacement property</u>. If a taxpayer files a federal income tax

return and reports a transaction as an exchange under § 1031, based on the

expectation that a dwelling unit will meet the qualifying use standards in section 4.02(2)

of this revenue procedure for replacement property, and subsequently determines that

the dwelling unit does not meet the qualifying use standards, the taxpayer, if necessary,

should file an amended return and not report the transaction as an exchange under

§ 1031.

.06 <u>Limited application of safe harbor</u>. The safe harbor provided in this revenue procedure applies only to the determination of whether a dwelling unit qualifies as property held for productive use in a trade or business or for investment under § 1031. A taxpayer utilizing the safe harbor in this revenue procedure also must satisfy all other requirements for a like-kind exchange under § 1031 and the regulations thereunder.

SECTION 5. EFFECTIVE DATE

This revenue procedure is effective for exchanges of dwelling units occurring on or after March 10, 2008. No inference is intended with respect to the federal income tax treatment of exchanges of dwelling units occurring prior to the effective date of this revenue procedure.

SECTION 6. DRAFTING INFORMATION

The principal author of this revenue procedure is J. Peter Baumgarten of the Office of Associate Chief Counsel (Income Tax & Accounting). For further information regarding this revenue procedure contact Mr. Baumgarten at (202) 622-4920 (not a toll free call).

SCHEDULE E
(Form 1040 or 1040-SR)

Department of the Treasury
Internal Revenue Service (99)

Supplemental Income and Loss

(From rental real estate, royalties, partnerships, S corporations, estates, trusts, REMICs, etc.)

► Attach to Form 1040, 1040-SR, 1040-NR, or 1041.
► Go to *www.irs.gov/ScheduleE* for instructions and the latest information.

OMB No. 1545-0074

2019

Attachment
Sequence No. **13**

Name(s) shown on return

Your social security number

| **Part I** | Income or Loss From Rental Real Estate and Royalties | Note: If you are in the business of renting personal property, use Schedule C (see instructions). If you are an individual, report farm rental income or loss from **Form 4835** on page 2, line 40. |

A Did you make any payments in 2019 that would require you to file Form(s) 1099? (see instructions) . . . . . ☐ Yes ☐ No
B If "Yes," did you or will you file required Forms 1099? . . . . ☐ Yes ☐ No

1a Physical address of each property (street, city, state, ZIP code)

A
B
C

1b Type of Property (from list below)	**2** For each rental real estate property listed above, report the number of fair rental and personal use days. Check the **QJV** box only if you meet the requirements to file as a qualified joint venture. See instructions.		Fair Rental Days	Personal Use Days	QJV
A		**A**			☐
B		**B**			☐
C		**C**			☐

Type of Property:

1 Single Family Residence   3 Vacation/Short-Term Rental   5 Land   7 Self-Rental
2 Multi-Family Residence   4 Commercial   6 Royalties   8 Other (describe)

Income:	Properties:		A	B	C
3 Rents received	**3**				
4 Royalties received	**4**				
Expenses:					
5 Advertising	**5**				
6 Auto and travel (see instructions)	**6**				
7 Cleaning and maintenance	**7**				
8 Commissions.	**8**				
9 Insurance	**9**				
10 Legal and other professional fees	**10**				
11 Management fees	**11**				
12 Mortgage interest paid to banks, etc. (see instructions)	**12**				
13 Other interest.	**13**				
14 Repairs.	**14**				
15 Supplies	**15**				
16 Taxes	**16**				
17 Utilities.	**17**				
18 Depreciation expense or depletion	**18**				
19 Other (list) ►	**19**				
20 Total expenses. Add lines 5 through 19	**20**				
21 Subtract line 20 from line 3 (rents) and/or 4 (royalties). If result is a (loss), see instructions to find out if you must file **Form 6198**	**21**				
22 Deductible rental real estate loss after limitation, if any, on **Form 8582** (see instructions)	**22**	(	)(	)(	)

23a Total of all amounts reported on line 3 for all rental properties	**23a**			
b Total of all amounts reported on line 4 for all royalty properties	**23b**			
c Total of all amounts reported on line 12 for all properties	**23c**			
d Total of all amounts reported on line 18 for all properties	**23d**			
e Total of all amounts reported on line 20 for all properties	**23e**			
24 **Income.** Add positive amounts shown on line 21. **Do not** include any losses	**24**		
25 **Losses.** Add royalty losses from line 21 and rental real estate losses from line 22. Enter total losses here .	**25**	(	)
26 **Total rental real estate and royalty income or (loss).** Combine lines 24 and 25. Enter the result here. If Parts II, III, IV, and line 40 on page 2 do not apply to you, also enter this amount on Schedule 1 (Form 1040 or 1040-SR), line 5, or Form 1040-NR, line 18. Otherwise, include this amount in the total on line 41 on page 2	**26**		

For Paperwork Reduction Act Notice, see the separate instructions.　　Cat. No. 11344L　　Schedule E (Form 1040 or 1040-SR) 2019

145

Tax Deferred Exchange Checklist and Documentation Requirements

1. _____ Suggested. Taxpayer adds Addendum to buyer's offer to show that transaction is a like kind exchange, and to allow contract to be assigned to Qualified Intermediary (QI).

2. _____ **Required.** A copy of the sales contract is faxed or sent to the QI with the name and phone number of the settlement agent/ attorney.

3. _____ **Required.** Taxpayer signs QI provided Exchange and Escrow Account Agreement, and Assignment of Contract prior to settlement. Signed documents are returned to QI. §1.1031(k)-1(g)(4)(iii)(B) and (4)(v).

4. _____ **Required.** Written notification of assignment is provided to all parties of the contract prior to settlement. §1.1031(k)-1(g)(4)(v)

5. _____ **Required.** Taxpayer keeps QI informed on any changes in closing date or the settlement agent/ attorney.

6. _____ **Required.** At settlement Qualified Intermediary receives exchange funds and places in qualified escrow account. Taxpayer has no control of funds. §1.1031(k)-1(g)(3)

7. _____ **Required.** Within 45 days of transfer taxpayer provides signed written notification to QI listing identified replacement properties. §1.1031(k)-1(b)

8. _____ Suggested. Taxpayer adds to replacement property contract Addendum to show transaction is part of a tax deferred exchange and that exchangor's rights may be assigned.

9. _____ **Required.** Taxpayer's rights in replacement property contract are assigned to QI prior to settlement. §1.1031(k)-1(g)(4)(v)

10. _____ **Required.** Written notification of assignment is provided prior to settlement to all parties of the contract. §1.1031(k)-1(g)(4)(v)

11. _____ **Required.** Within 180 days of transfer of first relinquished property Taxpayer must receive replacement property.§1.1031(k)-1(d)

12. _____ Authorized. At end of exchange period, QI provides any remaining escrow account funds, and interest earned to Taxpayer. §1.1031(k)-1(h)

13. _____ **Required.** Exchangor files IRS Form 8824 for tax year in which first relinquished property was transferred. IRS Publication 544.